2024 - 2025

No-Fluff Beginner Guide To

Cricut Maker
Projects

Easy Do-it-Yourself Profitable Cricut Projects and Design Space
Techniques

Volume 2

Linda C. Brown

Copyright

Copyright©2024 Linda C. Brown

Table of Contents

Chapter 1

Paper Crafts

Paper Lanterns

Materials needed

- o Cricut Machine
- o Heavy Cardstock (True Brushed Paper)
- o Standard Grip Cutting Mat
- o Cricut Weeding Tool
- o Cricut Scraper
- o Glue/Glue Dots/Tape
- o Glass Vase (optional)
- o Battery Operated Candles

Open the Cricut design space and tap on 'New project'. Tap on shapes and select a square.

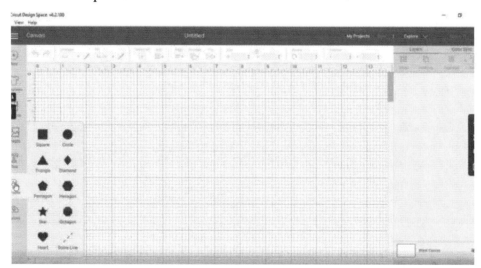

To change the measurement unlock it at the top menu. The paper lantern will be wrapped around a glass face. Make the lantern 11.5

inches by 7.8 inches. Change the color of the rectangle to gray for easy visibility.

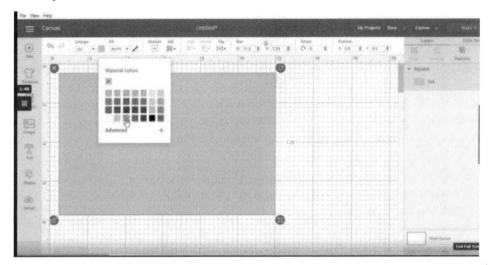

To add images to the lantern, go to the search bar and type "all images" in the Cricut design space. If you are a member of Cricut Access, you have access to thousands of images. I want to make a starry light lantern. I also want to include the moon so go to the search bar and type 'stars and Moon'.

Select the shapes you want and insert them into your canvas.

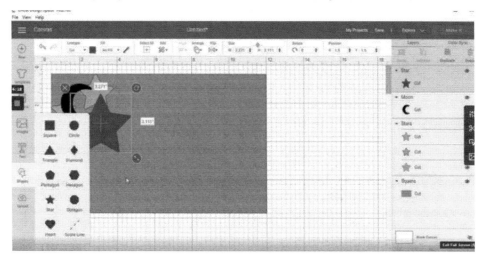

I want to add dots too so place them strategically on the lantern. Resize these three images and then select all and click duplicate as many times till the rectangle is full.

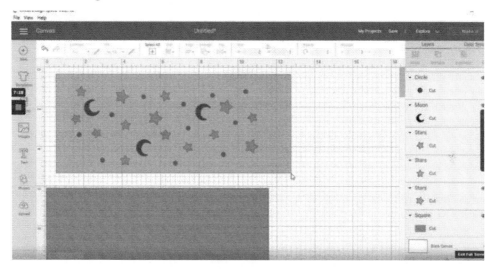

Remember to leave a 1/2″ margin on each side where the lantern will be glued. Select all images excluding the rectangle and tap 'weld' to put them together.

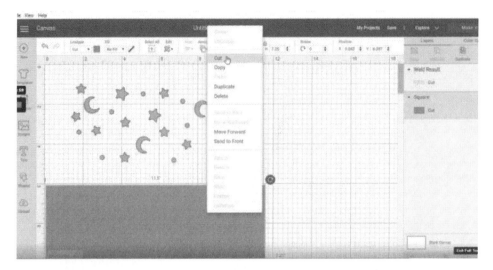

This transforms the individual images into a single entity, allowing you to slice through the rectangle shape. Click on the slice icon to cut through the shapes using the rectangle.

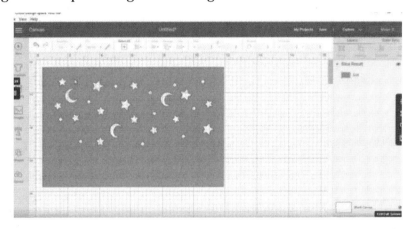

Click "Make it."

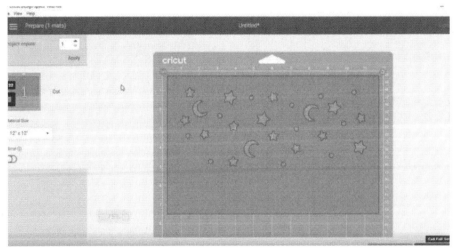

If everything looks good click "continue." Adjust your machine settings to cut Cardstock. Ensure the Deep Cut Blade is properly placed in your machine for optimal results with thick cardstock. Set the material you are using to custom. Position the cardstock on the standard green cutting mat

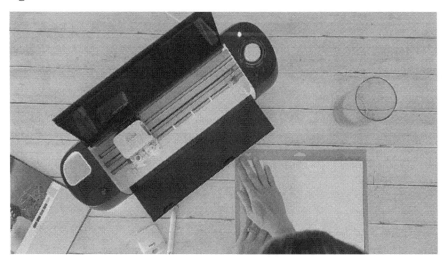

Place it in the machine.

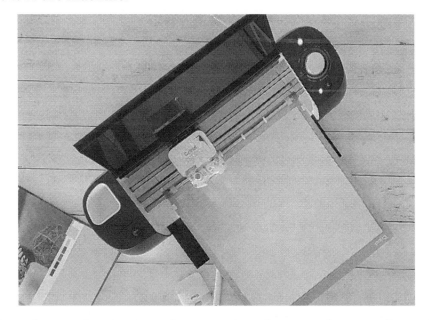

Initiate the cutting process by pressing the start button. Once done, carefully take the cardstock off the cutting mat to unveil your finished piece. Consider using a weeding tool to delicately remove intricate images, especially with the True Brushed paper's thickness.

If necessary, take a Cricut Scraping tool to detach the cardstock from the mat.

Wrap the cardstock around the glass vase for the Cricut lantern.

Take clear-drying glue, glue dots or clear tape to attach the paper lantern to the glass face then press down lightly.

If you are not using a vase, use tape on the inside and outside to attach the two pieces. Drop a battery-operated candle inside it.

Handmade Envelopes

Materials Needed

- o   Circuit machine
- o   Circuit mat
- o   Card stock

    o Glue

    o Scissors

Instructions

Open design space and start a new project. Select a square

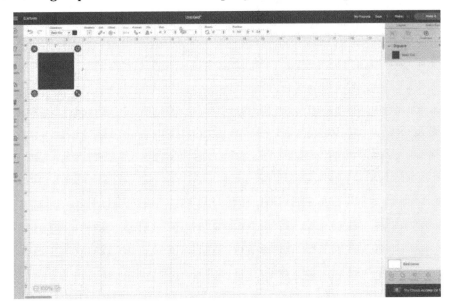

Make the square box 3 inches by 7 inches. Change the color to white and place it on the X and Y axis at 0.5 and 0.

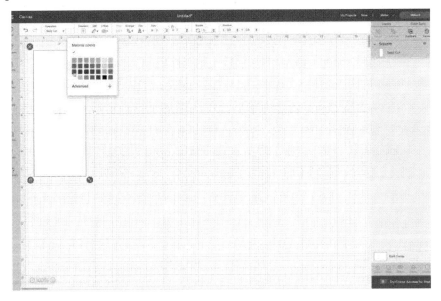

Make a flap that will be positioned on both sides of the square. Select a hexagon,

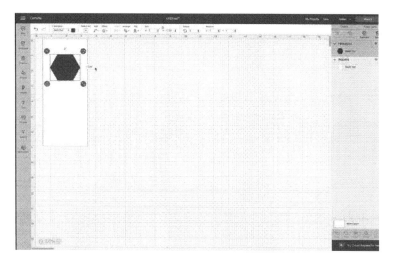

Place it at the Y at 5 and the X at 0. At this point, the size doesn't matter.

Select a square and place at X 0.5 and Y at 0.87. Both axis overlap at the point where I want to split or cut the shape. We only need the top section of the hexagon. Select both the hexagon and the square and click on the slice.

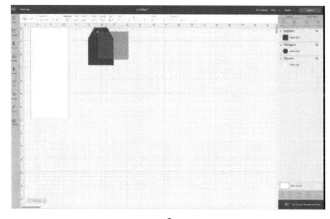

9

Remove the sections you don't need and delete. Here is the flap of the envelope. Change the color to white and make the size 3 inches by 0.5 inches.

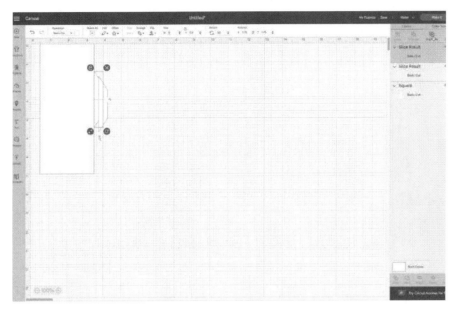

Rotate the flap at 90° and place it on the X at 3.5 inches and the Y at 1.5 inches. Duplicate the envelope and select all of it. Click on flip horizontal and place the duplicate on X at 4.5 inches and Y at 1.5 inches. Both flaps should line up on both sides of the square.

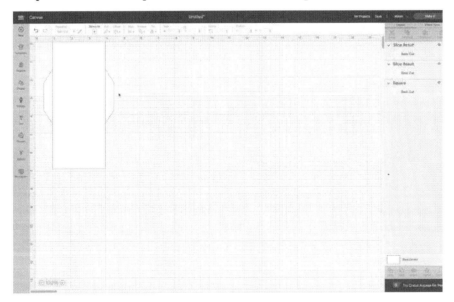

Select the images and click 'continue.'

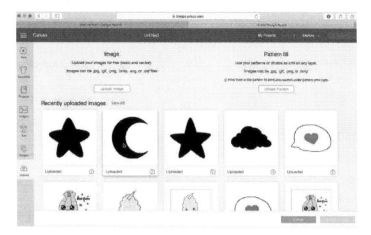

Click on the eraser tool to erase and make the images transparent. Tap 'continue' and keep it as an image for cutting.

Insert the image (star) and make it smaller by about 2 inches.

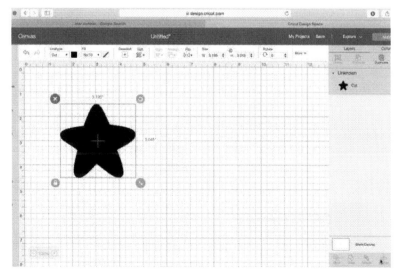

Duplicate the three images by copying and pasting them twice.

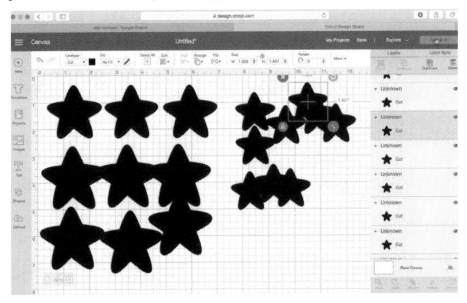

Repeat these steps for the moon and cloud. Click on 'Make it.' If everything looks good on the mat preview screen,

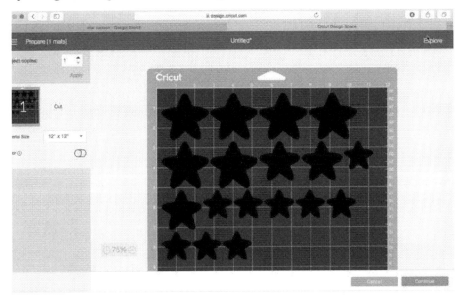

Click 'continue.' Set your materials and tools. Place the cardstock on a mat and put it into the circuit machine to cut. Remove your design and weed it. Cut three strings of about 31 inches, and evenly tie each string around the round metal until the strings can hold the round metal evenly.

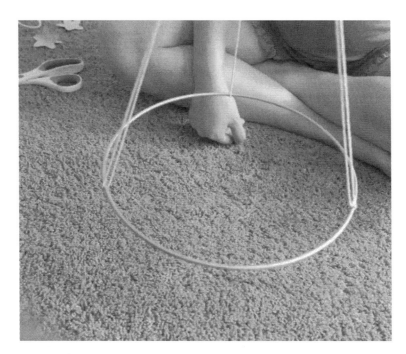

At the top, tie a knot.

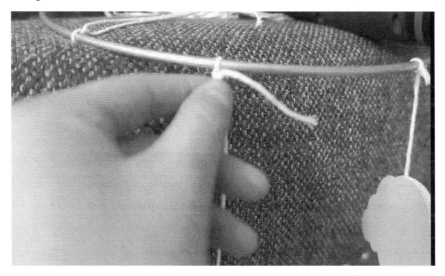

Take a single string of any length and tie it loosely around the round metal piece. The number of strings you choose to attach to the metal piece is entirely up to you. Personally, I tied six strings around the circumference of the round metal. Secure one string around the center where the three knots meet, ensuring it is positioned in the middle of the round metal piece. Begin hot gluing the shapes together by sandwiching them.

At the end of the string, attach a feather pom-pom or one of the themed decorations to close it off. Use invisible thread and a hook to hang it from the ceiling.

Origami Art

Materials Needed

- o Cricut machine
- o Cricut Standard grip mat
- o Regular cardstock
- o Wedding tool
- o Glue

Instructions

Open the design space, and click on a new project. Tap the shape icon and select a tall triangle.

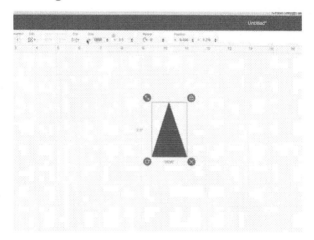

Resize it to one inch in width.

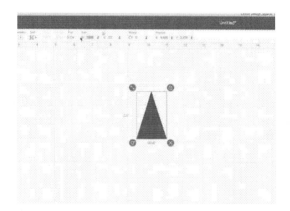

Copy another triangle from it, unlock the resize option, and edit the height to 3 inches.

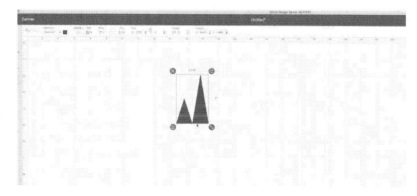

Next, highlight them and copy and paste a row of them until there are a total of eleven.

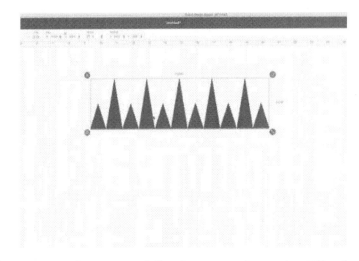

Copy and paste another row while the second row is still selected.

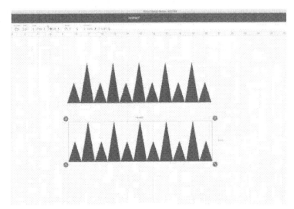

Choose vertical under the flip option at the top and position it below.

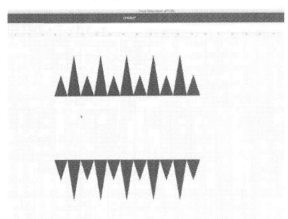

Select both rows together and ensure that the overall size of this design measures about 10.5 inches in width and height. Add a rectangle to fill the space in the center.

16

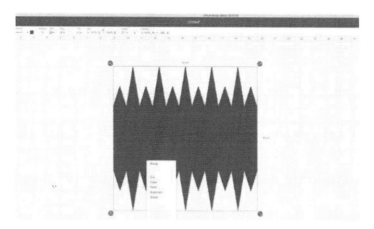

To combine all these pieces into one whole piece, select everything and click 'weld.' Change the color. Under shapes, choose a thin line option which is a scoring tool to create a scoreline where the star will be folded.

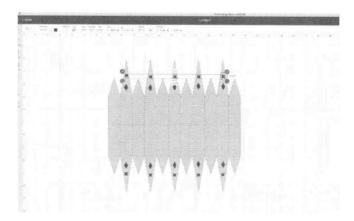

Go to shapes, select a diamond shape, resize to a thin diamond shape and line it up on top of the star.

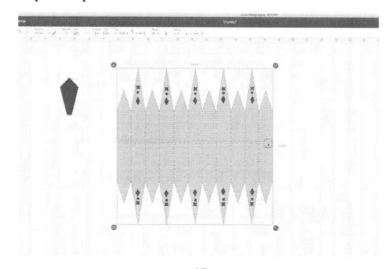

17

Copy and paste this design on the top of the design

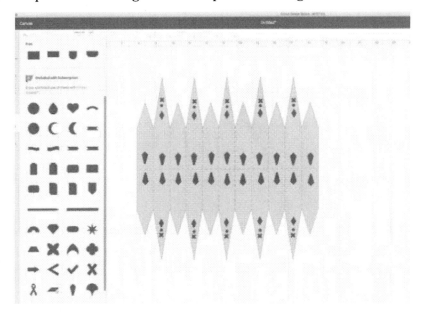

To do this hold shift on your keyboard and carefully click on the design. Use the keyboard shortcut command C to copy and command V to paste. Add a scoreline in the middle of the design. Under shapes, select a dash resize it, and carefully add a row of them along the scorelines.

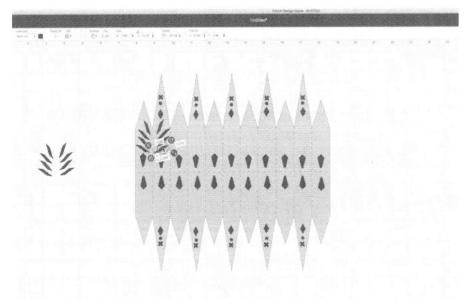

Choose the option cut on the mat. Set your materials and tools.

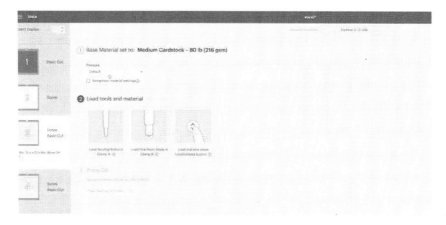

Put the material on a mat and place it in a machine to cut.

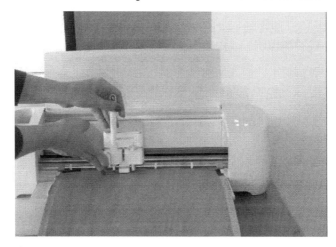

Remove the design from the mat.

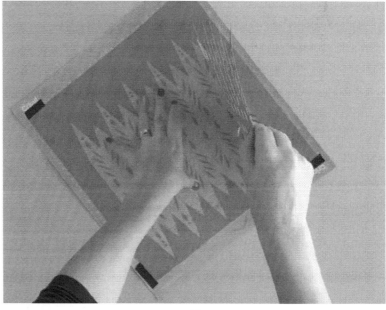

To assemble it, start by folding along the score lines just like folding a paper fan to secure in the center.

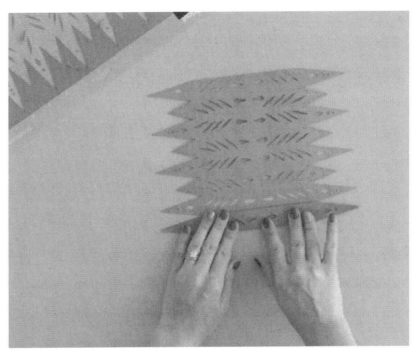

Take a floral wire and use the center of the score line as a guide, glue both ends together.

Spread out the stars a bit and glue the edges

Paper Quilling Designs

Creating your quilling paper strips with an electric cutting machine is a fast and straightforward process. Here are three different methods of cutting paper quilling strips.

Materials Needed

- o   Cricut machine
- o   Cricut light grip mat
- o   Laser copy paper
- o   Brayer

Method 1

Ensure you cut quilling strips with margins on both sides to prevent tangling. After tearing them off, trim the ends for a neat finish.

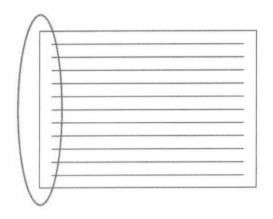

Method 2

Create quilling strips with fringe by leaving a margin on one side for ease of management. This method minimizes wastage compared to Method 1, making it suitable for scrap pieces rather than full-sized paper.

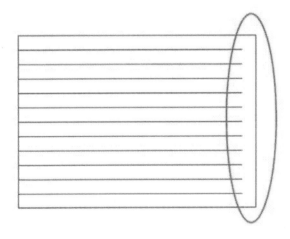

Method 3

Cut Quilling Strips Without Margins.

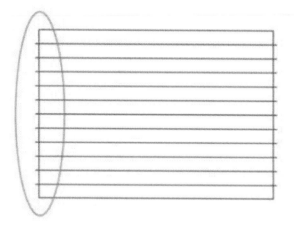

This cutting technique produces no waste because each strip is cut separately.

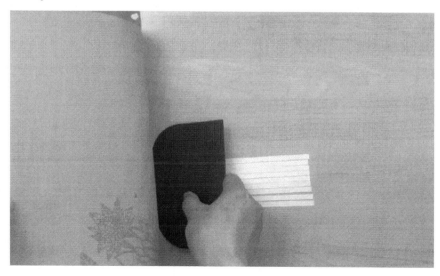

Chapter 2

Home Decor

Customized Throw Blankets

Materials Needed

- Cricut machine
- Cricut mat
- Cricut easy press or pressing iron
- Heat transfer vinyl (glitter iron on)
- Wedding tool
- Throw Blanket

Instructions

Open the design space and click on 'upload.' Go to upload images, browse and retrieve from your downloaded folder on your desktop. Click on the SVG to import it into the design space. Resize the image to about 11.5 inches wide to fit the throw blanket. Click 'weld' to put all the pieces together. Click 'Make It'. On the mat preview screen, select 'on mat', tap the mirror icon and click 'continue.'

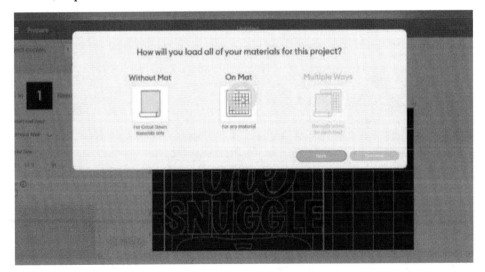

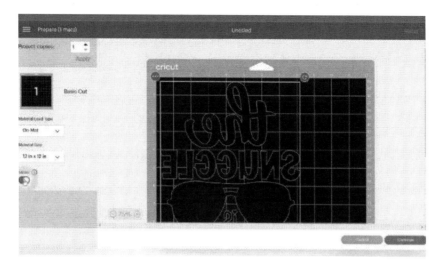

Set your base material to glitter iron on heat transfer vinyl.

Also, select and set the tools.

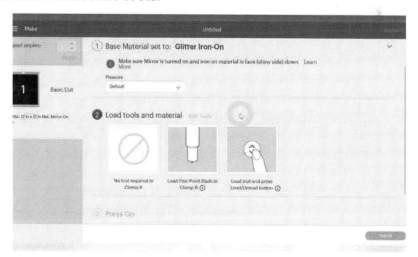

Place the vinyl on the mat and put it in the machine to cut. Take off the vinyl from the mat and weed the excess vinyl. Open the throw blanket and spread it out.

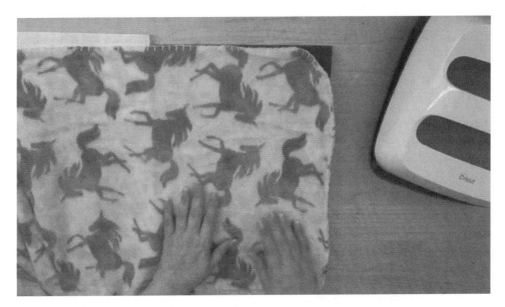

Make sure it is polyester. Polyesters are good for heat transfer vinyl. Place the design on any part of the blanket but I will place this in the bottom right-hand corner. Flatten the part of the blanket you want to apply the vinyl.

Turn on the cricut easy press and preheat it to about 320°. Place the design on the throw blanket, cover it up with a butcher's paper and put the cricut easy press on it for 15 seconds.

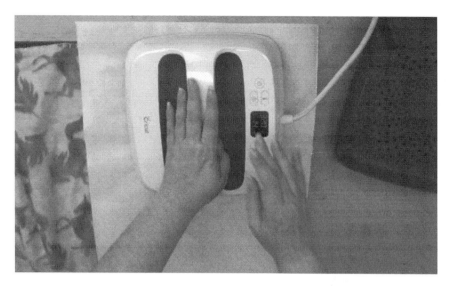

Press two times because the easy press did not cover the design, you have to do it in parts. Allow the design to cool and then peel off the tape.

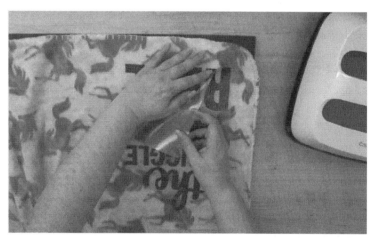

Your project is done.

Decorative Vases

Materials Needed

- o Glass vase
- o Vinyl in three different colors - light pink, dark pink, and teal*
- o Transfer tape
- o Tools
- o Cricut machine
- o Cricut tools - weeding tools, smoothing tool
- o Scissors
- o Light grip cutting mat

Instructions

Open the design space and choose a wildflower stencil pattern.

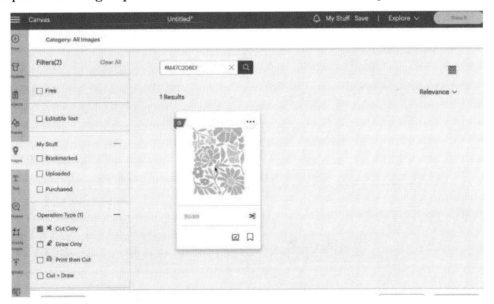

Rotate it to 90° and resize it to 5 inches by 11 inches.

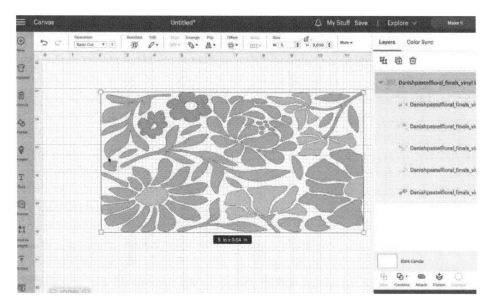

Change the colors of the layers.

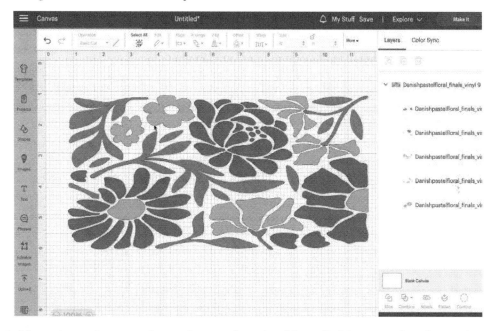

Add registration marks to layer the vinyl by clicking on the shape icon to insert a triangle beneath your design adding a couple of triangles one for each color of vinyl, such as green, light pink, and dark pink in your case.

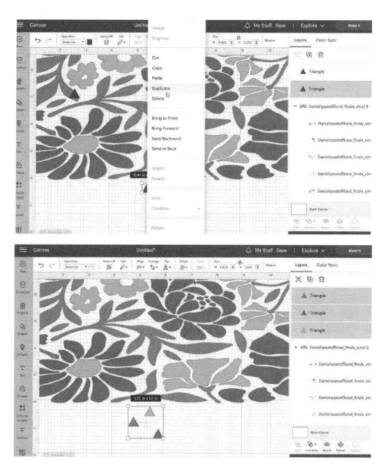

Select all three triangles and click on "align center" to stack them directly on top of each other. Create a copy of this stack and position it two inches to the right of the original. Align them to be on the same plane, click "center vertically," and nudge them up and next to your pattern.

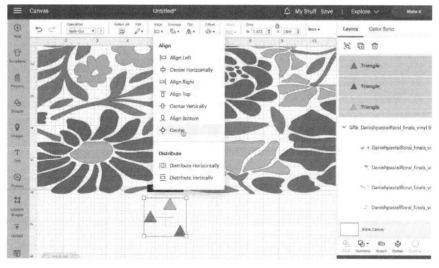

Select each element of the same color and unite them together so that when you cut it, everything is arranged correctly.

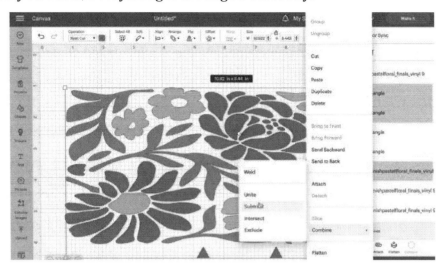

Click 'Make It'. Preview the mat screen and click 'continue.'

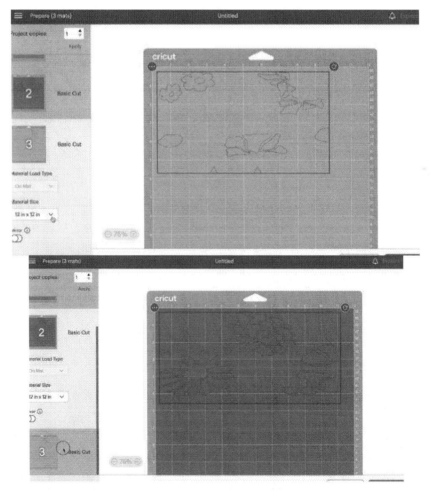

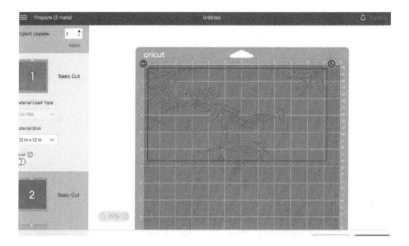

Set your materials and tools. Place the vinyl on the mat and put it in the machine to cut. Remove the vinyl from the mat and weed your designs.

Place the transfer tape on the design to ensure that the transfer tape is on the same level as the registration marks. Use the scraper to smooth it out.

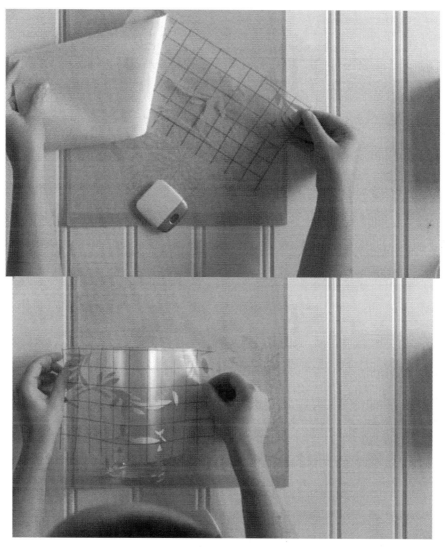

The glass vase is about 5 inches tall so place the first layer of vinyl. Line it up with the top edge of the vase. Start from the center and smooth it all the way around. There is an extra seam, smooth down one end of the vinyl and then peel back the transfer.

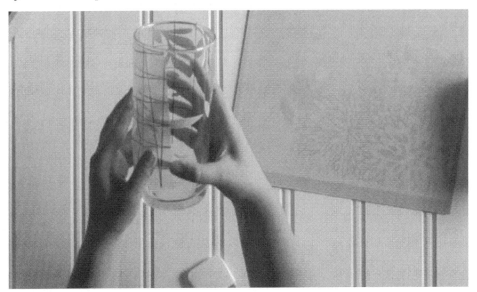

Repeat this same step for the remaining two layers of vinyl.

Complete the bottom of the vase by affixing a piece of solid vinyl.

Invert the vase, cut 1-inch slits in the excess vinyl, and fold each slit over the bottom of the vase for a finished look.

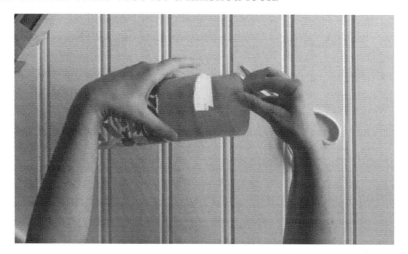

Your project is ready.

Personalized Wall Clocks

Materials Needed

- o Cricut machine
- o Cricut mat
- o Rotary cutter
- o Premium vinyl
- o Cardstock
- o Wedding tool
- o Scraper
- o Acrylic ruler
- o True control blade
- o Transfer tape
- o Small screwdriver
- o Denatured alcohol or rubbing alcohol (in a spray bottle)
- o Small bowl (to collect the screws)
- o Wall clock

Instructions

Remove the clock from the box and turn it over to remove all the screws at the back.

Pop the face of the clock out and set the pieces aside.

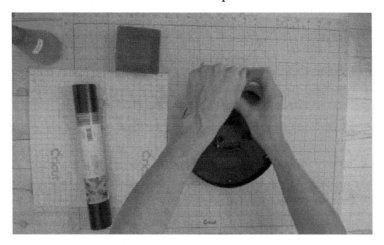

Remove the hands of the clock by lifting them one after the other. You are now left with the clock face (circle). Measure the circle. It measured 7.25 inches. Use the cardstock to cut it out.

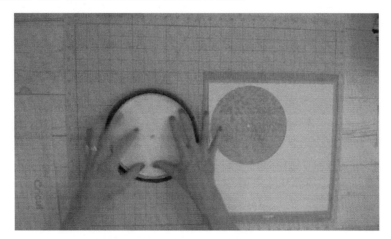

Open the design space and click on 'new project.' Tap on the shape icon and select a circle. Change the color to white. Resize this circle to the measurement of the clock face 7.25 inches. Tap on 'text' icon to bring in the text box. Type 'BEST DAD EVER'. Go over to don't and select a bold and thick font. Change the color of the text to the color of the vinyl you will be using. Rearrange into three lines and adjust the spacing between the letters and the words using the line and letter spacing icon on the top of the menu. Resize the words to fit into the circle. Click 'hide' to remove the circle and click 'make It'. Set your materials and tools. Cut a piece of vinyl using the rotary cutter, place it on a mat and use the washi tape to hold it firmly on the mat. Put the vinyl in the machine to cut.

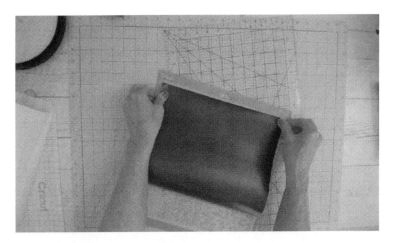

Remove the vinyl from the mat after cutting, use the true control blade to trim the vinyl, and a weeding tool to weed your design. Measure transfer tape enough to cover your design, peel off the paper backing and place it on top of the vinyl.

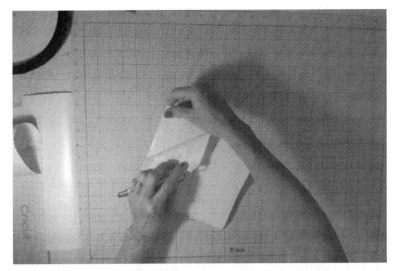

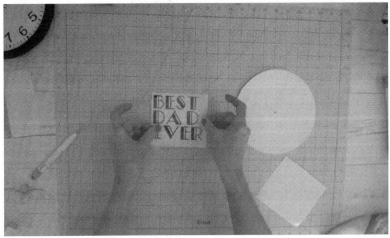

Use the scraper to smooth it down to remove all bubbles.

Gently lift the transfer tape with the design on it.

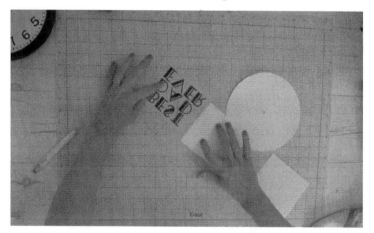

Place the transfer tape on the circle cardstock, use the scraper tool to smooth it down and peel off the transfer tape.

Use a little bit of glue to stick the back of the cardstock to the face to prevent it from popping out and hindering the hands of the clock from moving freely.

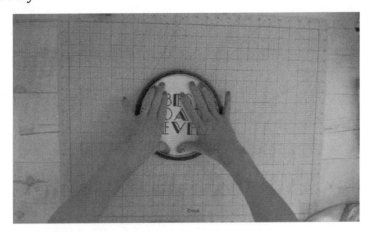

Reassemble the clock. Fix the hands of the clock, spray some alcohol on the glass to clean it, cover the glass, and flip the clock to put back all the screws. Ensure that all the screws are tightly fitted. This is the final look of the clock.

DIY Wreaths for Every Season

Materials Needed

- Cricut machine
- Cricut standard grip mat
- Medium Cardstock
- Textured paper
- Brasswood (wreath)

- o Wedding tool
- o Quilling tool/ tweezers
- o Hot glue scoring tool
- o Wool String

Instruction

Open the design space and click upload. Type easter eggs, bunny, leaves, rolled roses, and wreaths in the Cricut search bar one at a time. Select the images you want. Click 'add to canvas' to bring in the images.

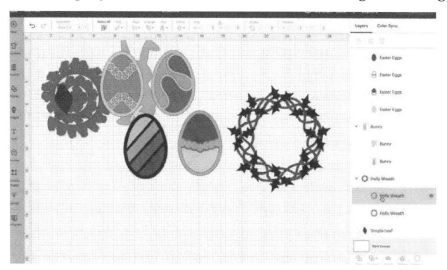

Layer the eggs to achieve a good thickness. Adjust the wreath circumference to 11.5 inches and change its color.

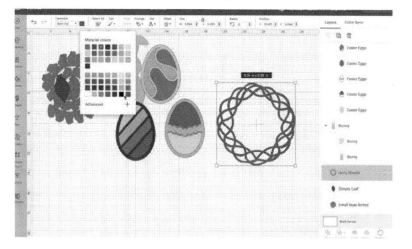

Ungroup the Easter eggs resize them to 3 inches and change their colors.

41

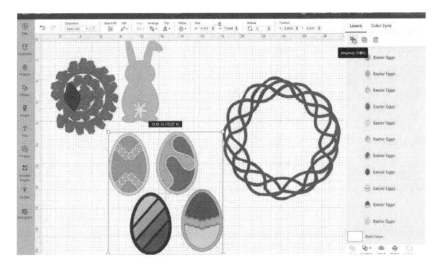

Click on the bunny to resize it too. Put the bunny, and the eggs on the wreath and resize again.

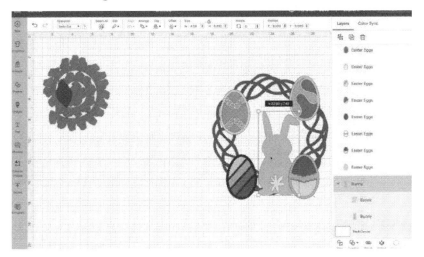

Click on the leaf to resize and duplicate it as many times as you need.

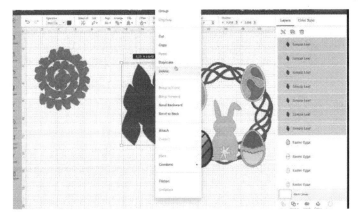

Resize the rolled roses to 5.5 inches and tap duplicate eight times.

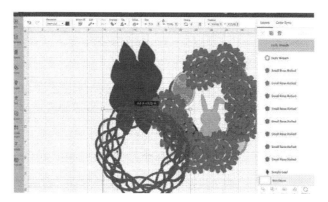

Duplicate the wreath.

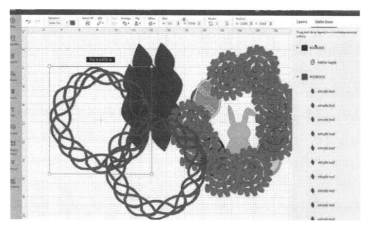

Set your material to basswood and ensure the deep int blade is placed in the machine. Place the basswood on the mat and place it in the machine to cut. Remove the wreath from the mat. Place the cardstock on a mat and place it to cut. Do the same for the bunny and the rolled rose. Remove the design from the mat and weed your design. Use a quilting tool or tweezers to roll the roses.

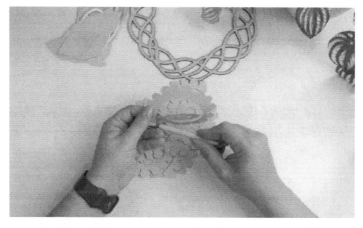

Secure the roses with glue at the center circle of the bottom.

43

Bend the leaves a little at the center using a scoring tool.

Glue the layered eggs one layer at a time and add rhinestones to one of the eggs.

Heat the glue gun and start organizing where each item will be. Put a little glue on the tail of the bunny and stick it to the wreath. Also stick the eggs, the rolled roses and the leaves.

Glue a string at the top of the wreath for hanging it to a wall.

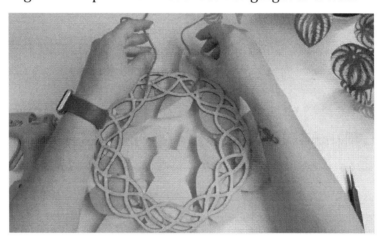

Chapter 3

Apparel and Accessories

Customized Socks

Materials Needed

- o Cricut machine
- o Cricut standard grip mat
- o Cricut easy press mini
- o Heat transfer vinyl
- o Scraper
- o Wedding tool
- o Two pairs of socks

Instruction

Open the design space canvas and click on the text icon. Type 'If you can read this'. Click on a font to change the text font style. Adjust the line spacing to bring it closer together.

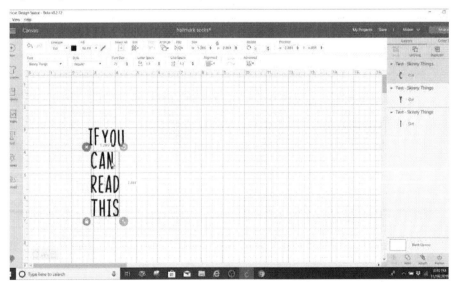

Highlight the top row and click 'align.' Highlight the entire words and click 'center horizontally' to group the words. Highlight the entire words again and click 'attach'. Click on the text icon and use the same font to type the second word 'Leave me alone I'm watching a Christmas movie.' Adjust the line spacing between the words.

I will add the Hallmark logo towards the end of the word. Go to Google and type 'hallmark logo'.

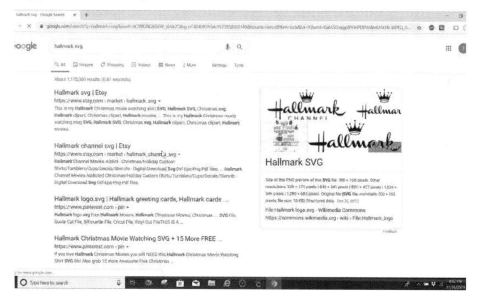

Click on images.

Select the first one. Copy and save images.

Go to uploads and upload the image. Click on 'complex' and go to contour to remove the crown.

Resize the Hallmark to be smaller and line it up with the second word. Highlight the Hallmark and click 'center horizontally.'

Resize the entire word to a height of 4 inches and a width of 2.5 inches. Highlight both words and tap 'attach'.

Click 'Make It'. This brings you to the mat preview screen. Mirror your design and click 'continue.'

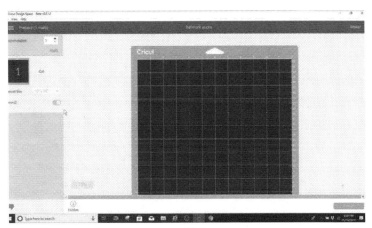

Set your materials and tools

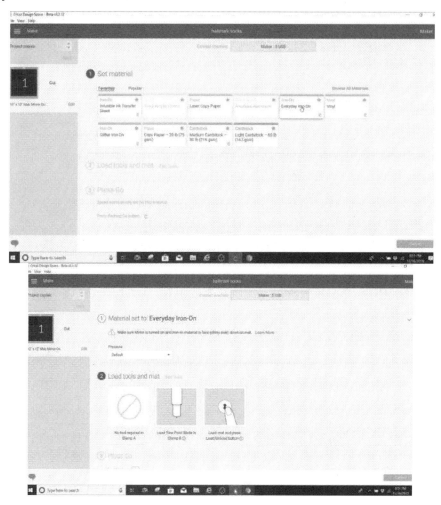

Place the heat transfer vinyl's shiny side down on the mat and put it in the machine to cut.

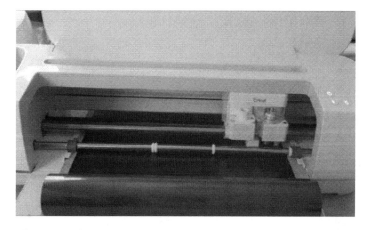

Weed your design after cutting.

Go to the Cricut heat guide to set the easy press mini. Click on 'Sports Flex' and select 'Polyester.' Set the heating time to 25 seconds.

When it is heated up, preheat both pairs of socks. Remove the carrier sheet from your design and place it on the socks.

Heat press for 20 minutes. Allow to cool for a few minutes and peel off the tape.

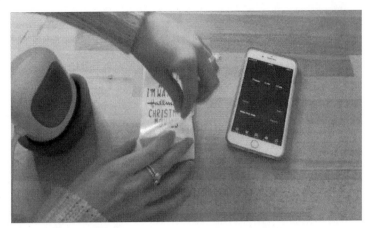

A final look at the project.

Embellished Jeans

Materials Needed

- o Cricut machine
- o Cricut standard mat
- o Printer (inkjet)
- o Heat transfer paper
- o Heat transfer vinyl
- o Cricut easy press
- o A pair of pants (jeans)

Instructions

Go to Cricut design space and click on 'Uploads.' Type 'flowers' in the search bar of the Cricut to choose a flower of your choice. Save the image.

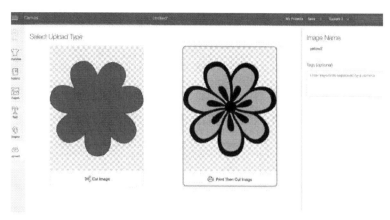

Click on the flower and tap on 'add to canvas'.

Resize the flower and click 'duplicate.' Resize the duplicate to be smaller and change the color to red.

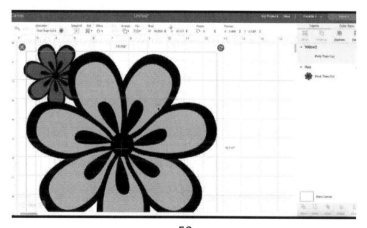

Set the image as print and cut. Save your design and send it to the printer to print. After printing, place it on a mat and put it in the Cricut machine to cut.

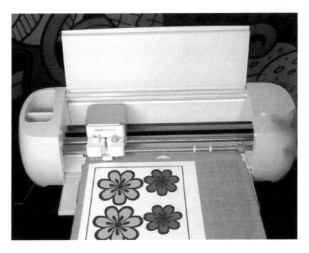

Remove the flowers from the mat. Preheat the jeans with the easy press and place the flowers where you want them to be before pressing them down.

Place the easy press on the flowers and press for 15 seconds.

Repeat this step for the other flowers and your project is ready.

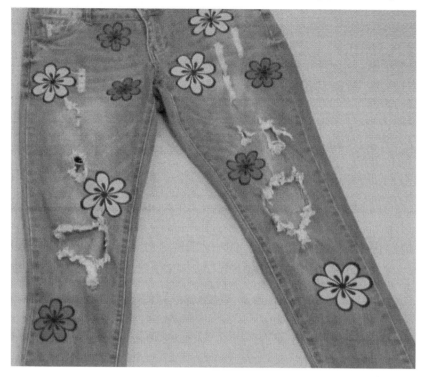

Handmade Hair Accessories

Materials Needed

- o Cricut machine
- o Cricut standard grip mat
- o Faux leather
- o Glitter bonded felt
- o Hair clips
- o Craft glue
- o Glue gun

Instructions

Go to Google and type unicorn head in the search bar. Select the image you want and download it. Save it on your desktop and then open the design space.

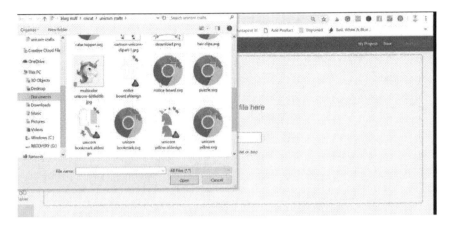

Click on 'new project'. Click on uploads and upload the image.

Browse for the file and click on 'save'.

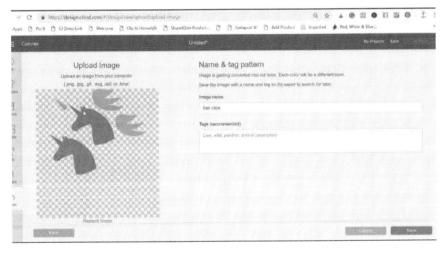

Click on the file and tap on Insert Image.

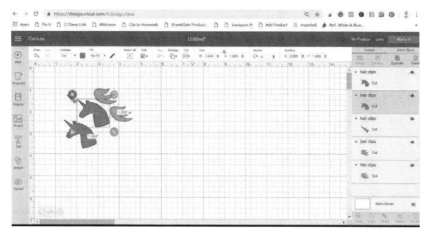

Go to 'ungroup' and flip one of the unicorns such that they are a mirror of each other. This will enable you to place one under the other. Flip one of the wings too and click 'make it'.

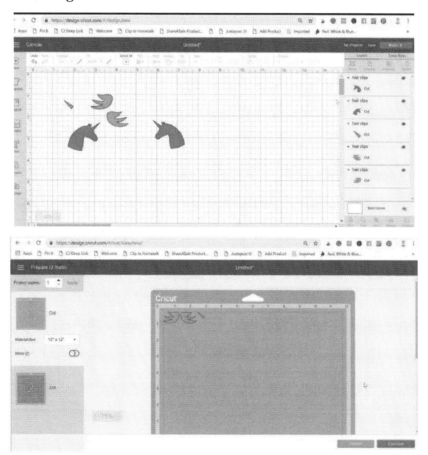

Click 'continue.' Load your mat, and set the base material as felt(I'm using glitter-bonded felt).

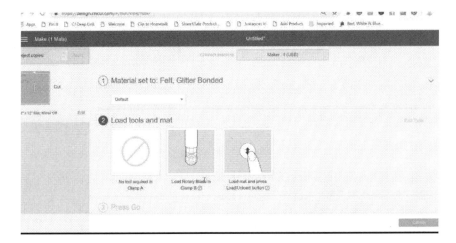

Select the faux leather paper thin.

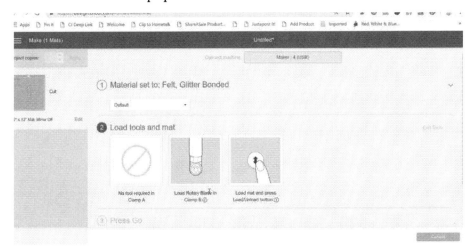

Click on 'more pressure.' Set the tool also (rotary blade)

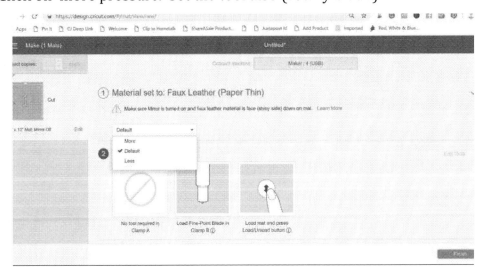

Load the mat in the Cricut machine to cut.

One of the unicorns and wings was cut with felt and the other with faux leather.

Start by gluing the wings on the unicorn.

Flip the other side, add glue and stick it on top of the hair clip.

59

Also, add glue to a smaller piece to cover the hair clip neatly.

Repeat this step to assemble the other unicorn hair clips.

Personalized Purses and Clutches

Materials Needed

- Cricut machine.
- Cricut mat
- Cricut permanent glossy vinyl
- Transfer tape
- Crossbody purse
- Rubbing alcohol
- Paper towel
- Scraper

Instruction

Open the design space and click on a new project. Tap on the text icon and select a font- cloud9.

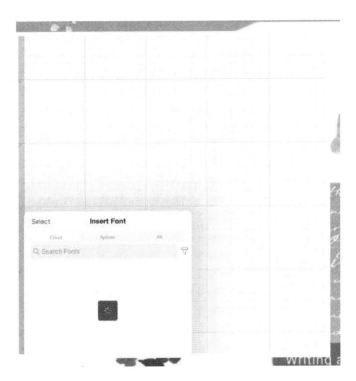

Type 'Cynt'.

Use the spacing icon on top to decrease the spacing between the letters or click 'ungroup' to manually move the letters closely.

Measure the front of the purse to know what size to make the word. Resize the word to 1 inch in height and 3 inches wide. Select all the letters and click 'attach'. Click 'make it' to preview the mat screen.

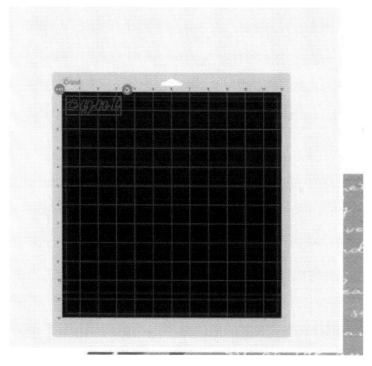

Set the materials and tools. Select premium vinyl and put the pressure on 'more' so it will cut all the way through.

Place the vinyl on a mat and put it in the machine to cut.

After cutting, remove the vinyl from the mat and weed your design.

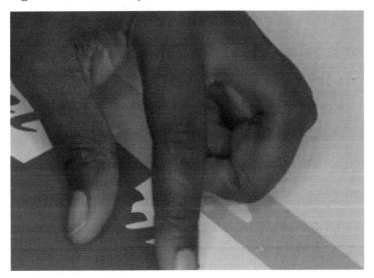

Cut a piece of transfer tape and place it on the vinyl. Smooth it out using a scraper. Peel off your design.

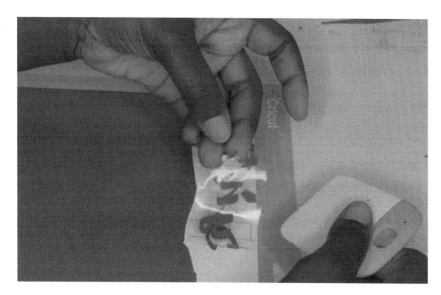

Use rubbing alcohol and a piece of paper towel to clean the surface of the purse before applying the vinyl.

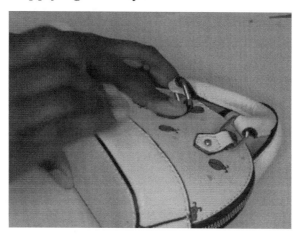

Place the vinyl on the purse, and use a scraper to smooth it down, removing all bubbles.

Gently peel off the transfer tape and your project is done.

DIY Sunglasses

Materials needed

- o Cricut machine
- o Cricut mat
- o Cardstock
- o Poster Board
- o Foil
- o Glue gun
- o Feeding tool

Instructions

Open the design space and click upload to upload the cut file, drag and save it.

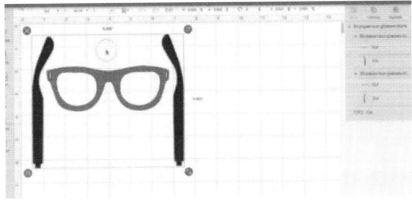

Resize the image. If you are making it for adults, resize it to 7 inches wide. For little children, resize to 3.75 inches to 4 inches, and for bigger children, resize to 5.75 inches to 6 inches. Resize to 4.75 inches. Go to the size icon and unlock it then type in 4.75. Click 'ungroup' and put in the score lines. Click 'attach' to attach the score line and the earpiece. Duplicate the glasses by copying them three times.

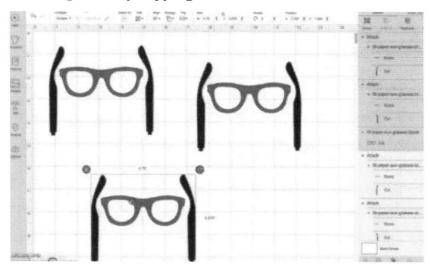

Click on text and select a font- Brooklyn. Type 'xoxo', 'be mine', and 'kiss me'.

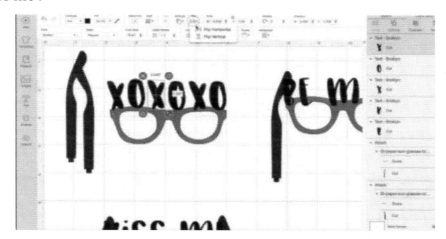

Resize the text. It is always better that the text goes a little bit outside the glasses so that it looks obnoxious. Adjust the spacing between each letter by clicking 'ungroup' to be able to move the letters closer together. Select all the text, click 'weld' and then select all the glasses, click 'weld' again and place them on each of the glasses. Now they are all one piece. Change the colors of the glasses to purple, pink, and orange.

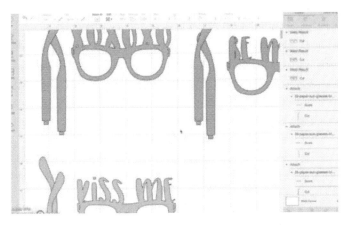

If there are any details on the glasses you don't want to be in the design, select the lettering on the sunglasses and click on 'slice'. Then tap 'weld' to put it back together again as one piece. If everything looks good, click,' Make It'. Set your materials and tools. Place the material on a mat and insert it in the machine to cut.

Remove your design from the mat and assemble the glasses.

68

Carefully fold the edges of the earpieces and slide them into the eyeglasses frame, apply small drops of hot glue for attaching.

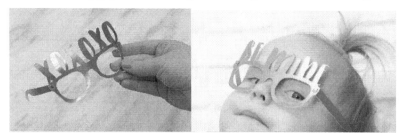

Chapter 4

Party and Event Decor

Personalized Party Hats

Materials Needed

- o Cricut machine
- o Cricut standard grip mat
- o Cricut weeding tool
- o Glue gun
- o Craft glue
- o Scissors
- o Cardstock

Instruction

Go to Creative Fabrics and download the 2021 New Year SVG file.

Change it to an SVG file and save it on your device.

Open the design space and click on upload. Double-click on the SVG to bring it into the design space. Before you go to upload, click on projects and search for party hats.

To begin the project, open your project and then import any additional images and fonts. Otherwise, you'll need to start over. Select the "celebrate" party hat and then tap "customize."

Here it is on your canvas but I don't want the 'celebrate' written on it. Click on the text and tap delete. Resize the hat to about 4 inches in width and then bring in your design.

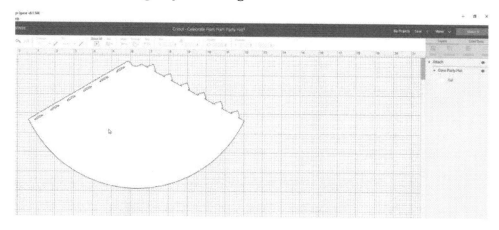

Click on "Uploads" and select the 2021 SVG file. Import it into Inkscape. Click on the 2021 to lock it and reduce its size to fit inside the party hat. Choose a color using the paint bucket tool. The color doesn't matter in the design space because you'll be adjusting the size. If you want to shrink it, you're creating an offset, so it will be smaller. In this case, you'll need to put a negative sign in front of it. However, if you want to enlarge it by 15, which will give you an outline, proceed accordingly. Click on the 202 and the shot, highlight them, and enlarge them by 30. Click on the paint bucket tool again to add color. Save the file as "2021 offset."

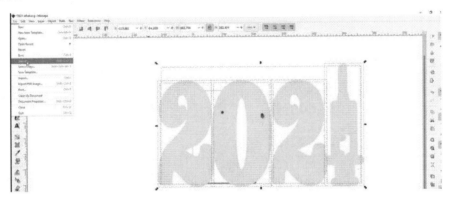

Go back to the design space and click on 'upload' image. Browse to find the file. Double-click on it and save it. And then click on it and insert it. Click 'Ungroup' to move the 2021 manually such that each number is touching and connected. Add more layers of offset to 2021. Highlight all images and click 'weld'.

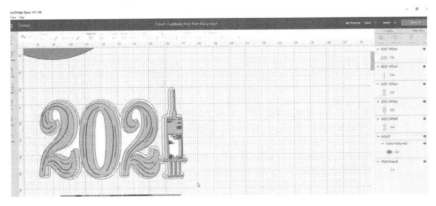

To remove any dots or lines you don't want to be part of the party hat design, go to contour and click hide. Place the 2021 inside the hat, increase the size of the hat to 6 inches and resize the numbers appropriately. You can use these steps for 2024, 2025, and any other year, if you wish to use this design.

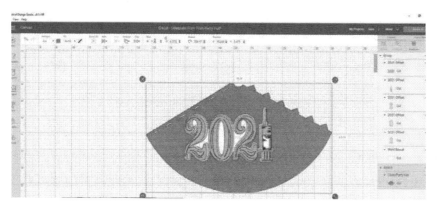

Tap 'Make It'.

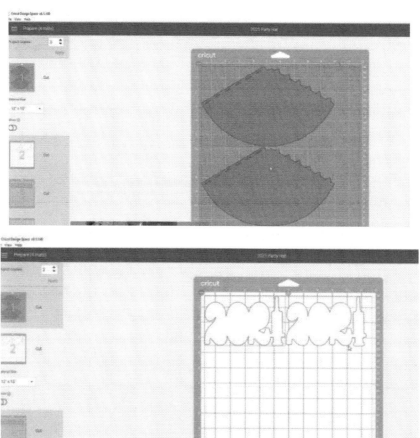

Send it to the Cricut to cut. Remove the design from the mat and weed your design. Apply glue on one layer of the 2021 and place over the other. Press down to stick. Place the 2021 piece on the front layer of the hat. Flip the 2021 piece put drops of glue and stick it on the front layer of the hat. Allow a few minutes to dry. Apply glue on one side of the top layer and place it on one side of the back layer to form a complete circle. Fold the circle into a cone by overlapping the two edges and apply glue to seal it. The extent of overlap influences the fit of the hat.

Themed Cupcake Topper

Materials Needed

- o Cricut machine
- o Cricut mat
- o Inkjet printer
- o Cardstock
- o Hot glue gun
- o Craft glue
- o Toothpicks

Instructions

Go to Google and type 'toy story' theme (Infinity and beyond). Select the one you want, download and save it on your device.

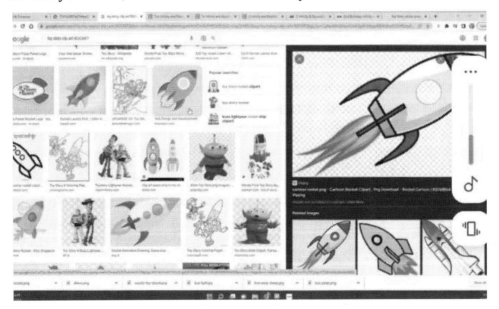

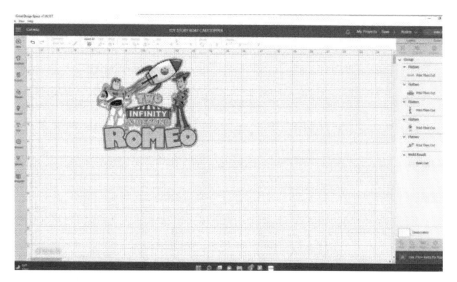

Open the design space and go to 'My Projects.' Select projects related to the toy story theme.

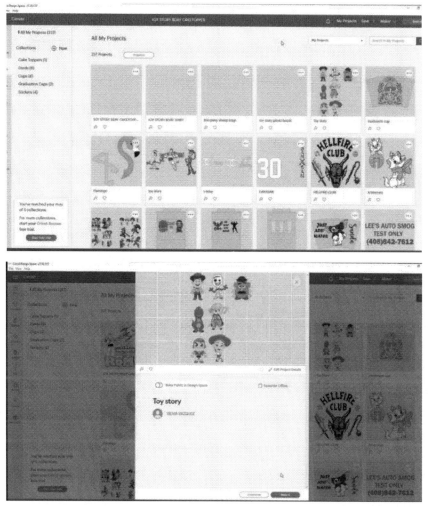

Click 'Customize' to import it into your design space canvas. Click on 'uploads.' Browse and select the 'infinity & beyond' svg. Click 'Add to Canvas' to see all your images inside the design space.

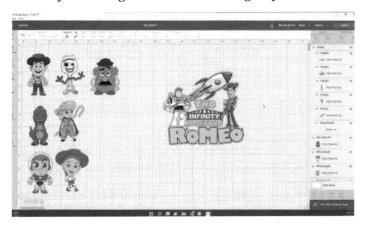

Click 'ungroup' to move the pieces manually and to remove anything you don't want. Delete the background and the cartoon characters beside the infinity image.

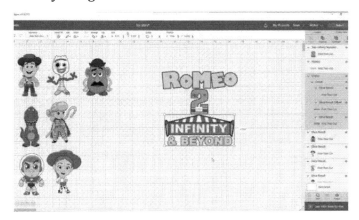

Adjust it to be bigger. Select everything and click on 'flatten.' Now it's one image. Create an offset and make the color white.

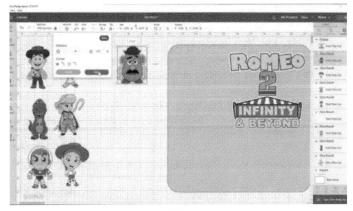

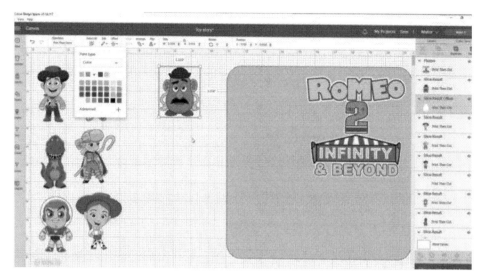

You can see it has an outline now. Highlight everything again and click 'flatten'. Also, add an offset to these images and click flatten. After adding the outlines to all the pictures. Insert a square and size it to be 6.75 by 9.25 inches. Then resize the images to be 5 inches in height. Click on attach to print everything as one.

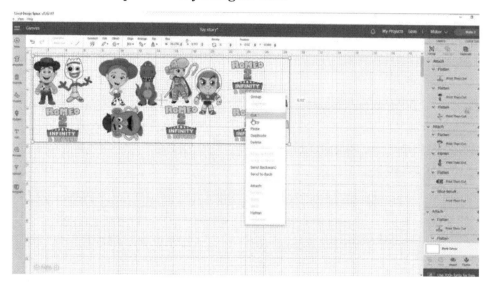

Highlight the images in the square and click 'duplicate.'

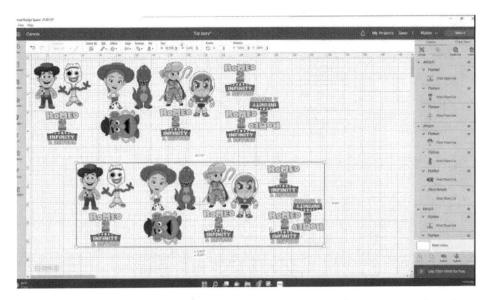

Here there are four pages in one and it measures about 9.2 inches by 6.73 inches. That means it will fit but each piece will be about 1 inch by 2.5 inches which will be perfect for cake toppers. Click attach again. Tap on the 'make it' icon. This will take you to the mat preview screen.

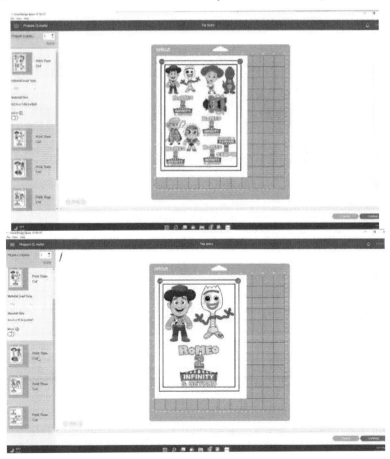

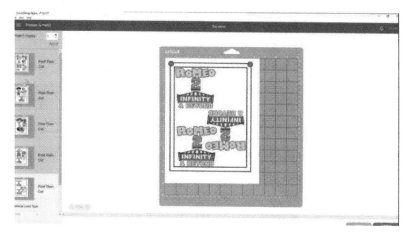

Send it to the printer to print and then place it on a mat and insert it in the Cricut machine to cut. Remove your design from the mat.

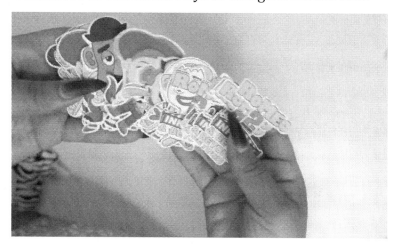

Flip the back of the cake topper and apply glue. Place a toothpick and allow it to dry.

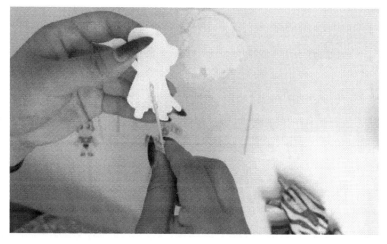

Repeat this step for all the cake topper pictures.

Customized Pinatas

Materials Needed

- o   A Cricut machine

- o   12x12 mat.

- o   Cardstock - 65 lb cardstock in pastels.

- o   Ribbon - approximately 3/8th of an inch and 3/4th of an inch in width.

- o   Craft glue

- o   Hot Glue gun and sticks

- o   Tweezers

- o   Candy, glitter, or confetti can be used to fill up your pinata!

Instructions

Open the design space and type 'Valentine's pinatas.' Select the one you want to make and click 'Customize.'

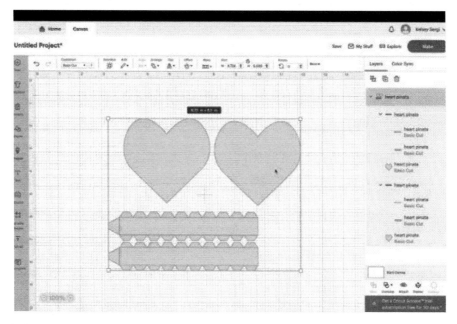

Click 'ungroup' to separate the entire file into individual elements and modify the lines on the rectangular pieces to either score lines or perforation lines based on the available tools. If the tools are unavailable, conceal or remove these lines. Ensure they are connected to the rectangles using the paper clip attachment feature.

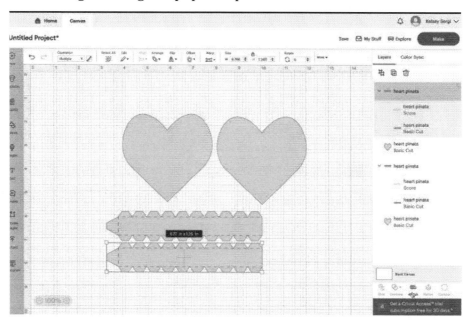

Adjust the size based on your paper dimensions and project preferences; Make it approximately a 5-inch heart with a total width of 11 inches, suitable for class cards or handouts for your children.

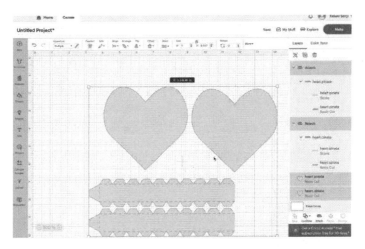

Click on the text icon to add text and tab on the font to select one. Type 'Hug Me'.

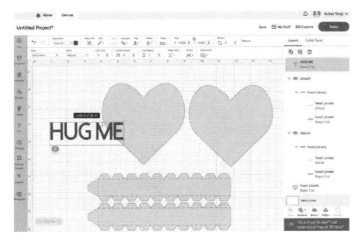

Make it into two lines, click 'ungroup', and adjust the spacing between the letters and the line manually. Click align and center. Change the color and tap on the weld to put the two words together.

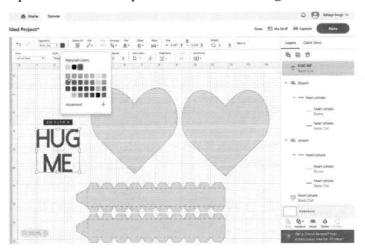

Place the text inside one of the hearts and resize them to fit.

Click on 'Make It to preview the mat screen.

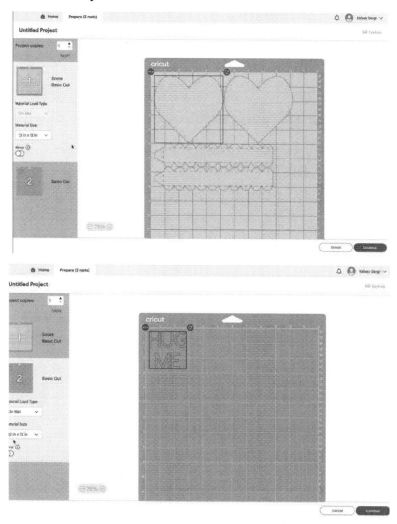

Set the material to cardstock and ensure the deep point blade and scoring stylo are inserted in the machine. Place the cardstock on the mat and insert it into the machine to cut. Attach your letters to the DIY piñata using glue.

Fold in the tabs, cut a ribbon strip that exceeds the length of one side.

Use hot glue to secure the ribbon along the full length of the side, leaving some hanging off the flat edge (without a tab).

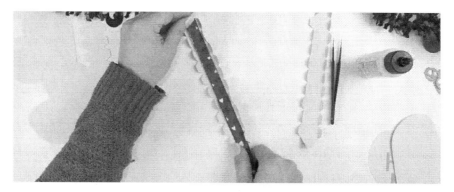

This extended portion serves as the pull string for hanging the heart. Trim the ribbon at the end to create a fishtail shape.

Apply craft glue to this side, working on a few tabs at a time, and let them dry. The ribbon's end should hang at the bottom point of the heart. Continue along the curve of the heart as you apply the glue and stick them together.

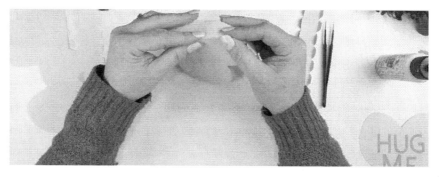

Fold the smaller piece of ribbon in half and secure it by gluing the ends together to form a loop. Attach this loop to the flat edge side of the other side piece, and ensure that it is hanging off the edge.

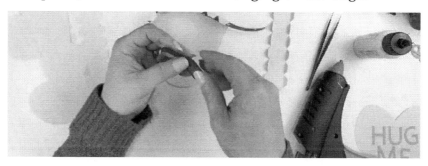

Secure this side to the other side of the heart using glue, working with a few tabs at a time.

Place the looped ribbon at the top center to serve as the pinata's hanging point.

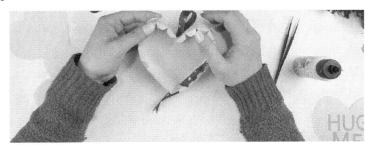

Attach the flap of the side piece to the other side at the top using glue, leaving the bottom unglued.

Fill your DIY pinata with confetti. candies, etc.

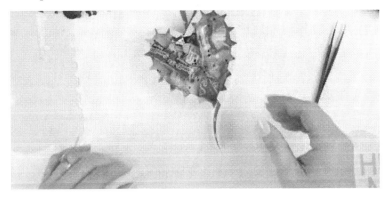

You can also fill it with a small coloring book and a few crayons. The choice of contents depends on the size of your pinata and the weight of the paper used in its construction. Repeat the same steps as earlier, gluing a few tabs at a time. Ensure thorough gluing, especially at the bottom point.

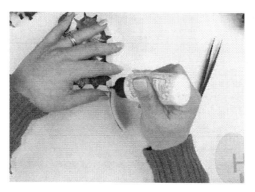

Maintain the side pieces pushed in for both visual appeal and added security. Let it dry completely before handling.

To open the pinata, pull the tab upward and rip along the side. Consider adding a small tag that says "pull me" or even "rip me" along the side of the DIY pinata.

Decorated Balloons

Materials needed

- Cricut machine
- Cricut mat
- Balloons
- Holographic Vinyl (blue, white, pink, and red)
- Measuring tape
- Transfer tape
- Scraper

o   Wedding tool

Instruction

Open the design space and tap on the text icon. Type 'Happy Birthday', 'Party', 'Lily' and 'Sophia.'

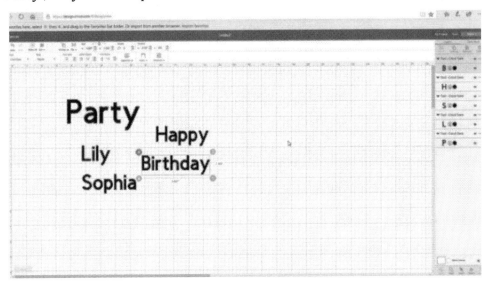

Tap on 'party' and change the font to Samantha. Reduce the letter spacing using the letter space icon so that the letters overlap. If you still need to adjust the spacings go to 'advance' and tap 'ungroup' to move the letters manually until they overlap nicely.

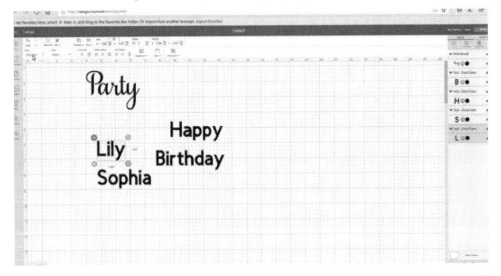

Tap on 'Lily'. Change the font and adjust the spacing between the letters such that they touch each other.

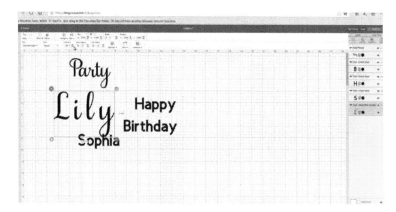

Tap on 'Happy Birthday and Sophie'. Change the font, reduce the spacing between the letters to touch each other and resize to fit the balloon.

Adjust the happy birthday to be able to stay on one balloon. Make the text to be on two lines. Highlight the happy birthday click align and tap center horizontally to maintain that gap in the middle. Highlight the text again and click on weld. Inflate one of the balloons and measure the curved surface. Use a measuring tape to measure around the front middle section. It is about 8 inches.

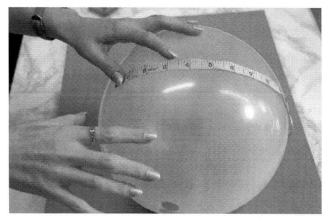

Resize your texts to fit in the respective balloons you plan to apply them to.

Change the color of the text to the color of the vinyl you will be using.

Click on 'Make It'. Check the preview mat screen and click 'continue.' Set your materials to holographic vinyl and tools. Place the vinyl on the mat. Do not use a scraper to smooth it down because it will scratch or ruin the holographic vinyl. Use a fabric brayer instead. Place it into the Cricut machine. Remove gently from the mat and weed your design.

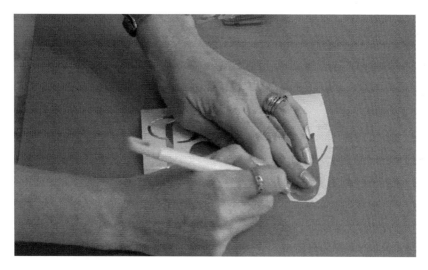

Place transfer tape over the design and use a scraper to smooth it down on the front and then on the back. Peel the design off from the back.

After transferring all the pieces to the transfer tape, use scissors to snip along the letters. If you are using a font that is not cursive, snip in the middle of the letters and do the same on the other side. Leave a small gap in between.

This will help you to position the vinyl on your curved surface. Bring the balloon and place the vinyl where you want it.

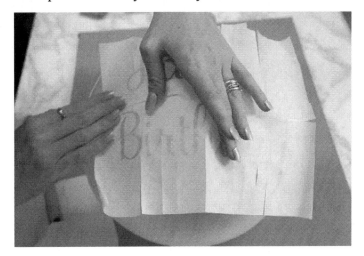

Start pressing down with the middle letter and then all the way outwards. Use the scraper to burnish it well.

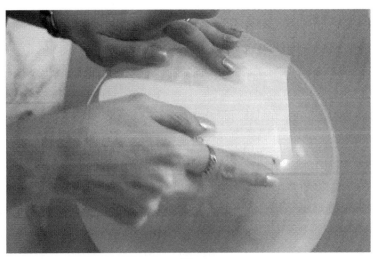

Gently peel back the transfer tape.

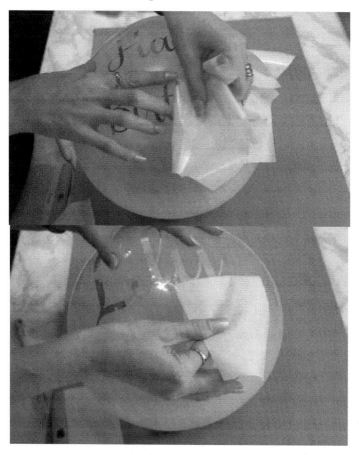

Repeat this step for the remaining texts on the balloons and your project is ready.

DIY Photo Booth Props

Materials Needed

- o Cricut machine
- o Canon printer
- o Medium cardstock
- o Cricut standard grip mat
- o Paper Straw sticks
- o Craft glue.
- o Hot glue gun

Instructions

Open a blank canvas on Cricut design space. Click on the left-hand side of the canvas to search for projects.

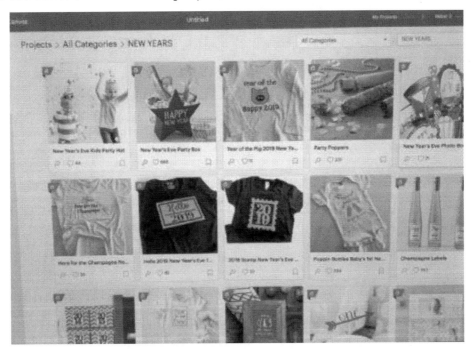

Type 'new year' and select the project of your choice.

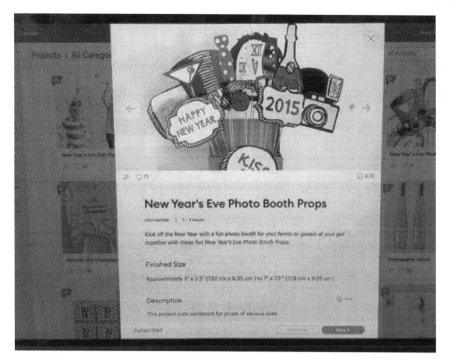

For this project, Cricut has a lot of instructions and materials you are going to need to cut and finish the project.

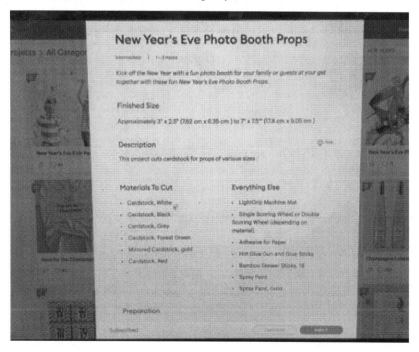

Instead, I will do a print and cut. That way, I can avoid cutting and gluing all these paper cardstocks. Click 'customize' to bring it to the blank canvas.

Click 'ungroup' and then tap on the martini and the glass. Highlight them and click the 'flatten' button at the bottom of the screen.

This will change the images from basic cut to print and cut. Perform the same steps on each of the images.

Click 'make it' to bring you to the mat preview screen.

Press 'continue.' Ensure the printer is ready to print out all the images. Select the add bleed button so that it doesn't bleed out on the edges. Click 'print.'

After printing, go back to the design space and set the materials and tools. Select your base material - medium card stock.

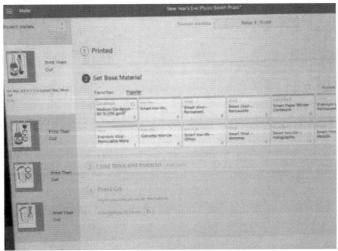

Put the cardstock down on a Cricut mat and load it into the machine.

Remove your design from the mat, weed and trim off the edges.

Take the lips and flip it over, apply a little glue and attach the paper straw.

Print two of each image and ensure you mirror one of them so that you can put the other one on this side. Attach a paper straw to the other images, and you are ready for the photo booth.

Chapter 5

Woodworking and Leather Crafts

Custom Wooden Signs with Leather Accents

Materials Needed

- Cricut machine
- Cricut standard grip mat
- Engraving tool
- Wooden frame
- Wood varnish
- Masking tape
- Folk antique wax
- Hot glue gun
- Craft glue
- Push pins
- Cardboard

Instructions

Take the folk art antique wax, a little bit of water to water it down and use this to paint or stain the frame. Make sure you use masking tape to line up inside corners to protect the inside part of the frame. When you are done staining the frame, take off the masking tape.

Open the design space, go to 'new projects' and type 'leaf'. Select one of the projects and click 'Add to Canvas.'

Resize the leaf to 5 inches by 7 inches.

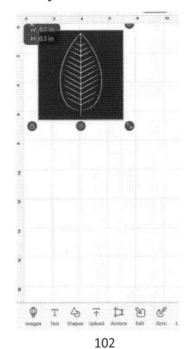

Go to 'operations' and click 'engrave'. This slightly changes the color.

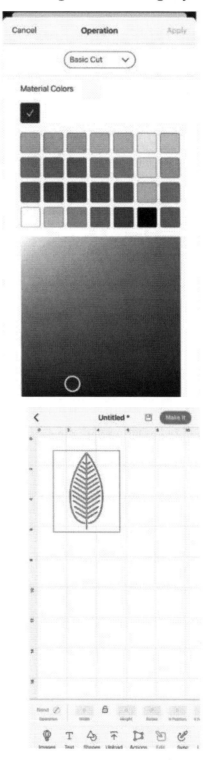

Select 'Make It' to view the mat screen.

If everything looks good, click 'continue.' Set your material and tool. Set the material to faux leather paper-thin and insert the engraving tool into clamp B.

Place the leather on a mat and place it in the Cricut machine to cut. Remove from the mat after cutting and trim down the rough edges to be nice and straight so it can fit perfectly into the frame.

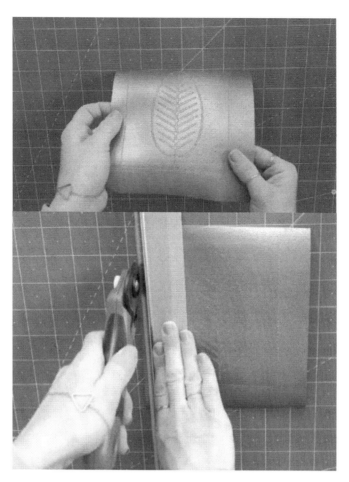

Cut a piece of cardboard and place the leather leaf design on the cardboard with Mod Podge.

Allow it to dry.

Apply hot glue in the middle of the frame and place the cardboard with the design on it. Cut off the head of a push pin, apply hot glue to it, and place it at the four corners of the leather.

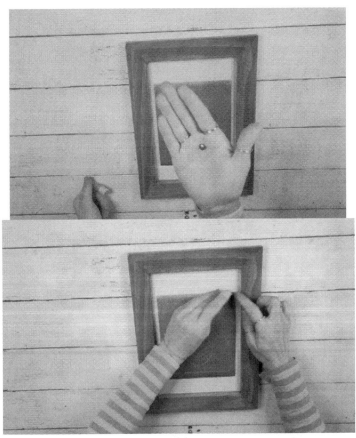

This is the final look of the frame.

Leather Bookmarks

Materials Needed

- o Cricut machine
- o Cricut standard grip mat
- o Textured leather
- o Faux leather
- o Painter's tape

Instructions

Open the design space, click on the shapes icon, and select the rounded corner rectangle.

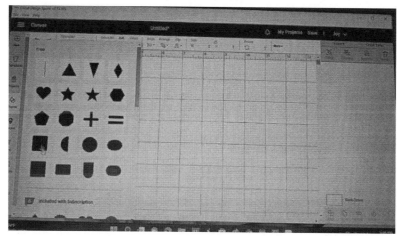

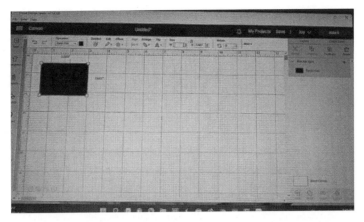

Resize the rectangle at the top of the bar to 1.5 inches wide by 4 inches high. Unlock this size.

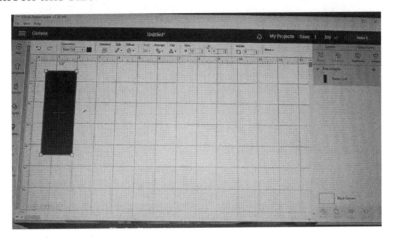

Select another rounded rectangle and resize it to be a bit smaller than the first. This will be the art of the bookmark hanging out from the edge.

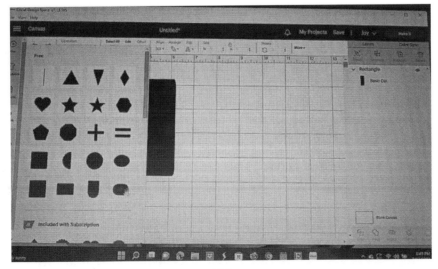

Add little circles to cut at the upper right corners of one piece and on the bottom right of the other piece. I will not be punching a hole for the string or ribbon after cutting the bookmark.

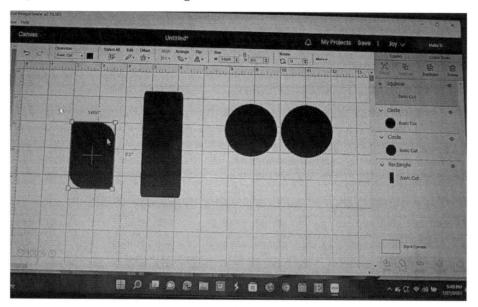

Add color to the circles and duplicate it. Place the circles far enough away from the edge of the leather so that it doesn't tear and not too far into the circle.

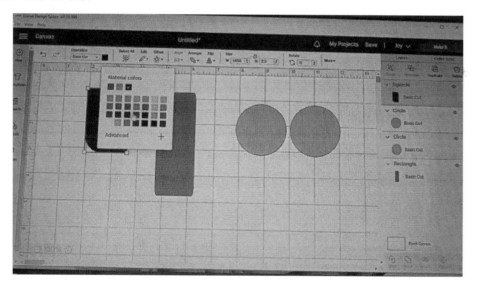

Highlight the two pieces, click 'slice' and 'attach' and then pull them away. After doing this, you will see purple and yellow circles on the right-hand side, they are no longer needed. They are the pieces that I cut off. Click on them and tap 'delete.'

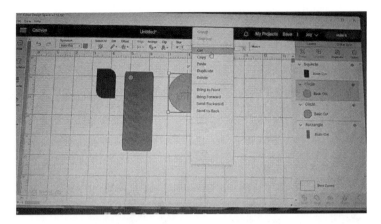

Highlight both pieces and click the 'slice' again.

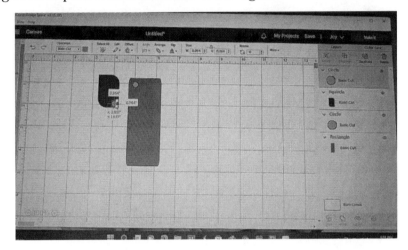

Both circles are no longer needed. Highlight and click delete.

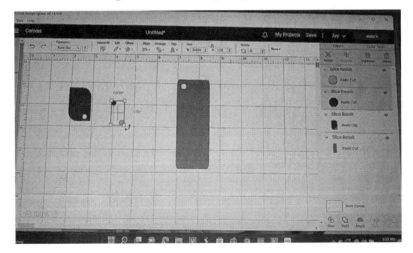

Click 'Make It'. Set your materials- faux leather paper thin and tools. Set the machine to more pressure. Place the leather on the mat, use tape to hold it down firmly, and put it in the machine to cut.

110

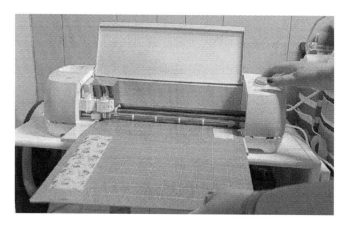

Peel off the tape gently and remove the leather from the mat. Remove the excess leather and knock out the tiny circles.

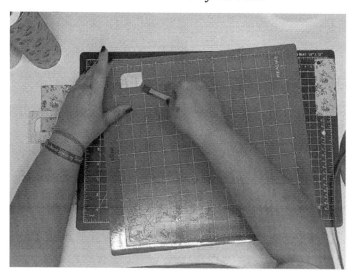

Take a string and do a double layer. Tread it into the holes of the bookmark and tie a knot nicely.

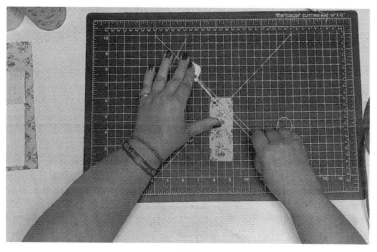

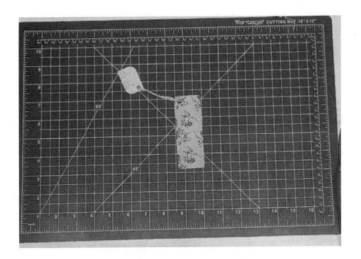

Leather Plant Hangers

Materials Needed

- Cricut machine
- Cricut strong grip mat
- 12 inches x 12 inch Cricut leather sheet
- 8 flat washers, 0.75 inch diameter
- 4mm-5mm cord
- 2 inches-3 inches ring
- Contact cement (like E6000)

Instructions

Open design space and click on the shape icon.

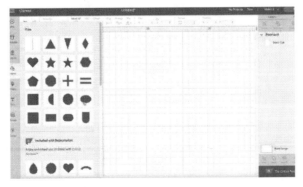

Select two ovals. Adjust the width of each oval to match the diameter of the base of your pot. Resize the length of the oval to be equivalent to the base of the pot plus a distance at least twice the desired height of the hanger sides. This distance can be influenced by personal preference, the thickness of the leather and the size and weight of the pot.

The pot plant has a 3.5-inch bottom diameter, and I'm using Cricut's genuine camel leather, known for its softness. Given its conforming nature and the ceramic material of the pot plant, extend the hanger sides to about 4 inches up. Resize the oval width to 3.5 inches and the length to 11.5 inches.

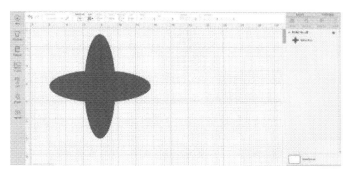

Click 'Make It'. Set your material and tools- utilize the deep point blade for cutting.

Position the leather's smooth-side-down on the cutting mat. This method enhances adhesion and keeps the mat cleaner. Particularly when using the entire leather sheet, it prevents star wheel marks at the ends, placing them on the opposite. Arrange the ovals perpendicularly, ensuring they are centered, and click 'weld' to put the shapes together as one piece. Click 'Make It'. Set your material - leather and tool- deep point blade. Place the leather in the mat, put it in the machine to cut. Remove your design from the mat and trim off rough and excess leather. Create holes approximately 0.5 inches from the edge at the end of each flap with a standard paper hole tool.

Apply glue to attach a washer around each hole on both sides of the leather. Leave it to dry.

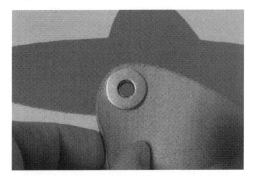

Trim two cord lengths to approximately 4 feet each, forming a hanger with a total length of around 2 feet. Adjust cord lengths for a longer or shorter hanger as desired. Fold the cords in half and thread the folded end through the ring.

Draw all four ends over the ring and pass them through the loop, forming a lark's head knot on the ring.

Thread one cord through the hole in each of the four flaps. Consider using tape on the cord ends to facilitate threading through the holes.

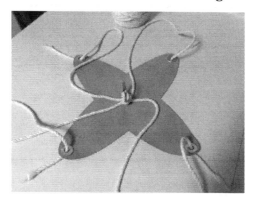

Secure an overhand knot at the end of each cord, ensuring the knot rests on the outside of the hanger.

Seat the pot in the hanger and assess its balance. Adjust and re-tie the overhand knots as necessary to achieve a balanced pot position. Once you are happy with the pot's hanging alignment, tighten the knots as much as possible.

Leather Coasters

Materials Needed

- o Cricut machine
- o Cricut standard grip
- o Sewing machine
- o Heat transfer paper
- o Pressing iron
- o Leather
- o Craft glue
- o Butcher's paper
- o Clean towel
- o Thread
- o Scissors

Instructions

Open the design space, click on the shape icon, and select three circles.

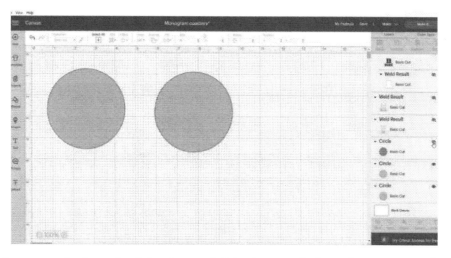

Resize one circle to be big about 4.3 inches and the other two circles to be small about 3.75 inches.

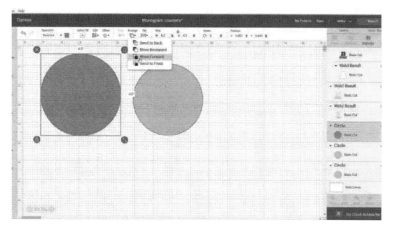

Align them such that the small circle is in the middle and the large circle is outside. The big circle is the base of the coaster and the little circle is the coaster.

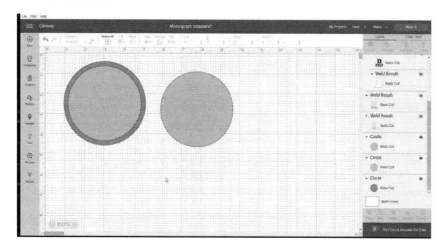

Click 'hide' to hide the small circle, adjust the size of the bigger circle to 4.5 inches to enable you to sew around in the base of the outer layer and then click 'Make It'.

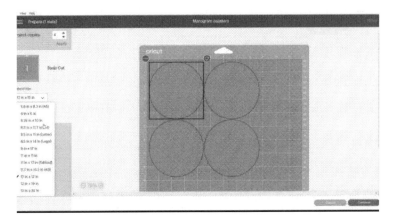

Set the materials to leather and tools to the knife blade.

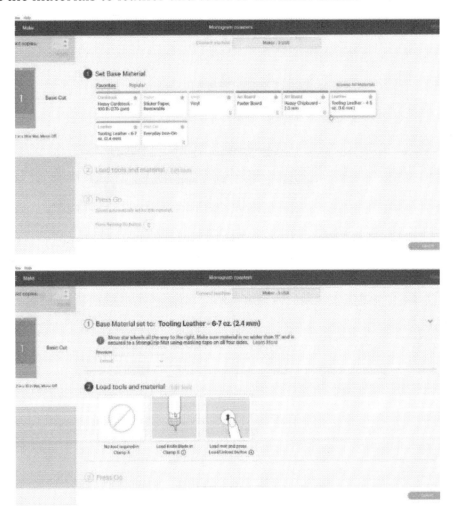

Put the leather on the mat, and place it in the machine to cut. Go back to the design space unhide the little circles and hide the big circle.

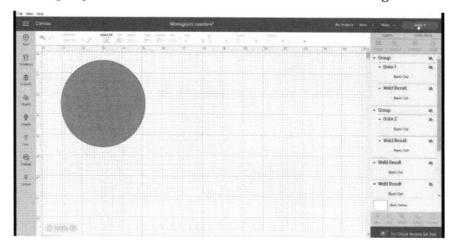

Align them the way you have your material and then click on the leather.

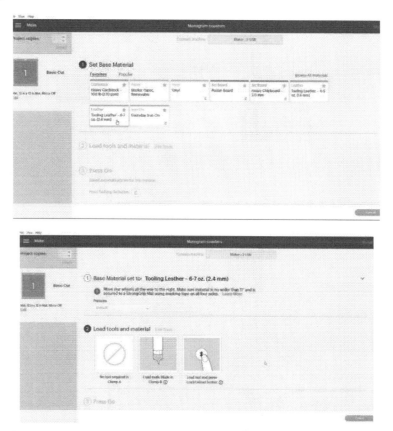

Put the leather on the mat, secure it with tape, and place it in the Cricut machine to cut. Ensure you have two circles of both the big and small ones. After cutting remove the design from the mat and detach it from the excess leather. Apply glue on the wrong side of the leather and place the wrong side of the other coaster to it.

Press until both stick together.

Use a clean towel to wipe off any excess glue sipping out of the edges. Top stitch around the tip of the coast using a sewing machine.

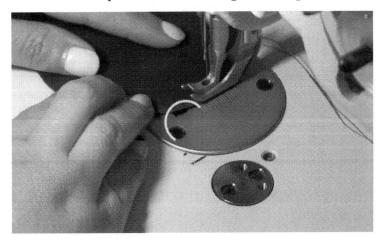

This is to make sure you have a finished look and also to hold both leathers strongly Do this for both the big and small circles. Use letters to personalize the casters. Design and cut out Duke and W with heat transfer paper with the Cricut machine. Heat the pressing iron. Place the Duke on the coaster, cover it with butcher's paper and put the iron on it for 30 seconds.

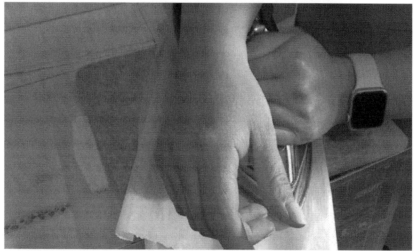

Make a strip of leather, this will be the edge of the coaster holder with the big circle. Measure a quarter of an inch from the edge of the strip and glue it.

Add clips so that you can fold it in place.

Do the line at half an inch so that you will have enough room to sew at the top stitch of the leather. Ensure the glue is holding both leathers down and wipe off any glue sipping from the edges.

Do a top stitch on the top, bottom and sides of the strip.

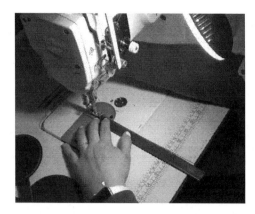

This is going to be around the big circle. Apply glue on the side of the strip and start pressing down around the edges of the big circle.

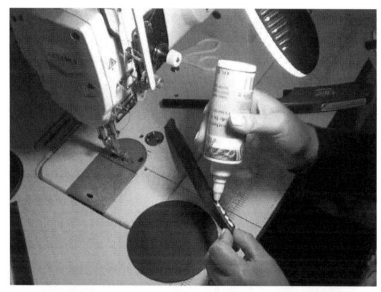

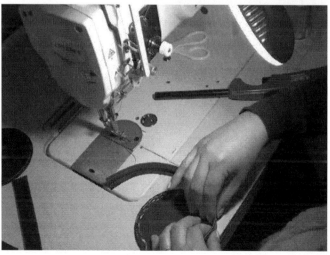

Top stitch the strip to the big circle.

123

The finished look of the coater.

Wooden Jewelry Holders

Materials Needed

- o Cricut machine
- o Cricut strong grip mat
- o Basswood
- o Hot glue gun
- o Craft glue

Instructions

Open the design space and click on the shape icon to select arches and circles.

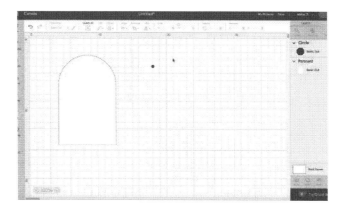

Place small dots for earring holes to create the main piece. Click 'weld'.

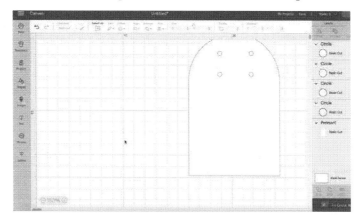

Click on the shape icon and select a quarter circle and a half circle.

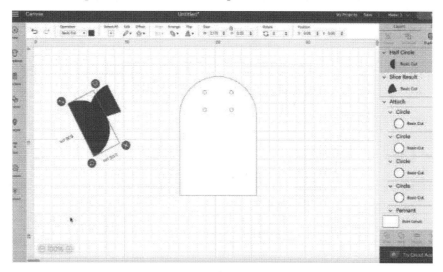

Overlay both circles to create the jewelry stand. Click 'weld'.

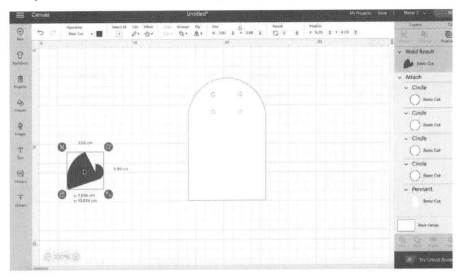

When you are done with the design, click 'Make It'.Set material, specifying the material type (chipboard 2mm) and ensuring the correct thickness for optimal results in this particular material. Set your tools-place the knife blade into the machine and set it within the Design Space settings. Confirm that the material being used is limited to a width of 27.5cm and align it with the top left corner of the adhesive area on the machine mat to avoid it passing beneath the star wheels. In case the wood extends under the wheels, trim it beforehand.

Securely tape all four sides of the wood to the mat, to prevent any slippage during the cutting operation. Put the wood into the machine.

After cutting the design, the machine will pause, allowing you to verify if it has successfully cut through. If not, you can proceed to follow the machine's instructions to execute more passes as needed. After cutting out the design, remove the wood from the mat and assemble the design.

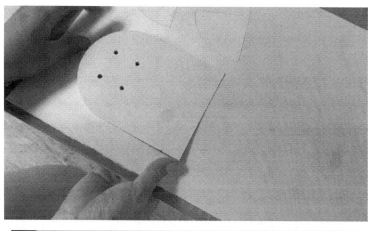

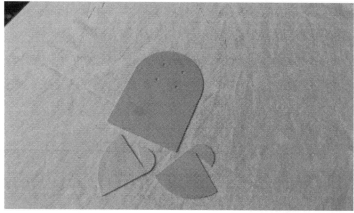

 Use stencil material to create a wave, stick it to the front, and apply paint.

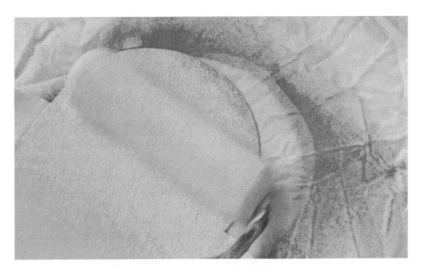

Allow to dry and remove the stencil material.

Secure the stands with a small amount of hot glue at the back to ensure stability.

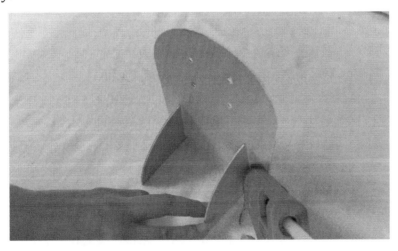

Your project is ready.

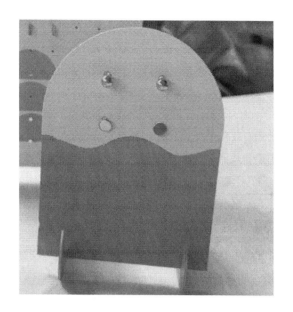

Chapter 6

Holiday and Seasonal Crafts

Personalized Christmas Stockings

Materials Needed

- o Cricut machine
- o Cricut standard grip mat
- o Wedding tool
- o Scraper
- o Heat transfer vinyl
- o Cricut easy press
- o Ironing mat
- o Parchment paper
- o Scissors

Instructions

Open the design space and click on 'new project'. Click on the text icon and type a name- Kobe.

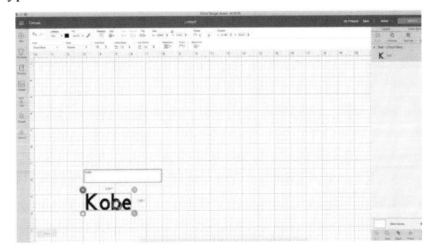

Drag the name up. Click on a font to select a script font- Lovina October.

Adjust the spacing between the letters to touch each other by tapping on the letter space on the top menu. Tap -0.5 to enable the letters to touch each other. Make the text size bigger. Measure where you want to place the name on the stockings. Make the text 7 inches wide. Click 'weld' to cut the text as one piece.

Go to uploads and search for images of paw prints. Select one and click 'Customize.'

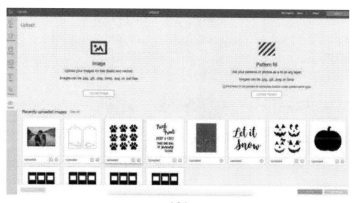

Resize them to fit the stockings. Select the entire paw prints and then click 'weld'. Add color to the text and image.

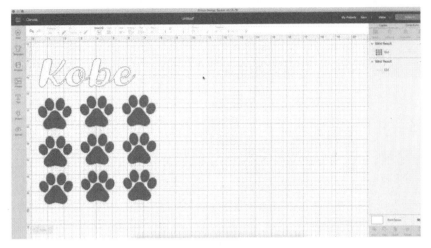

The name will be cut out in red and the paws in white. Click 'Make It'.

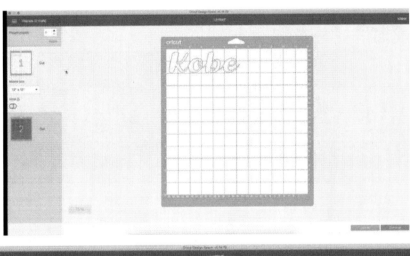

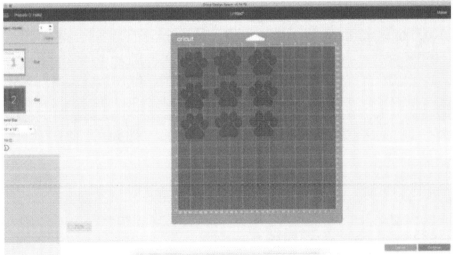

You will see two mats on the preview screen. One for the name and the other for the paw prints. Ensure the mirror icon is turned ON on the text mat preview screen. Click 'continue'. Set your material- heat transfer vinyl and tool. Place the heat transfer vinyl on a mat with the shiny side down and put it into the machine to cut. After cutting, remove the vinyl from the mat and weed your design. Cut out each paw and arrange them on the stockings.

Set the Cricut easy press to 220°. Place a parchment paper over the heat transfer vinyl and pit the easy press on it for 30 seconds. Allow it to cool before peeling off the protective backing. Put the parchment paper on the vinyl and place the easy press on the design again to make sure it sticks properly.

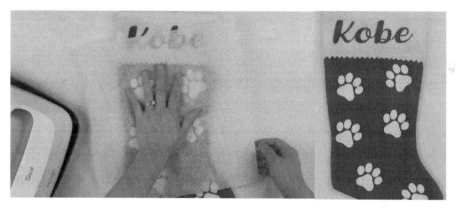

DIY Advent Calendars

Materials Needed

- o Cricut machine

- o Cricut standard grip mat

- o Brown paper bags(24)

- o Stickers
- o Clothespin
- o Cardstock (gold)
- o Advent gifts(24)
- o Craft glue
- o Glue gun

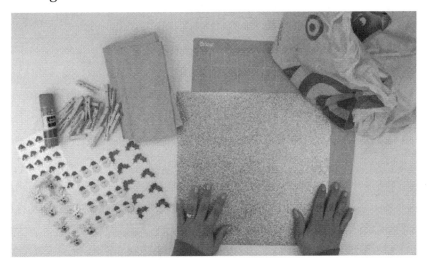

Instructions

Open Cricut design space and tap on a new project.

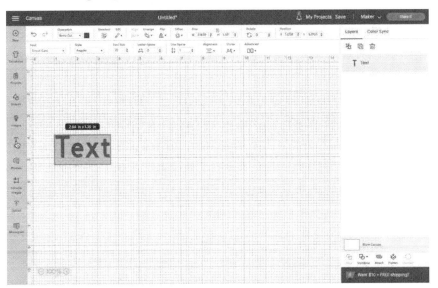

Click on the text icon and type numbers 1 through 24.

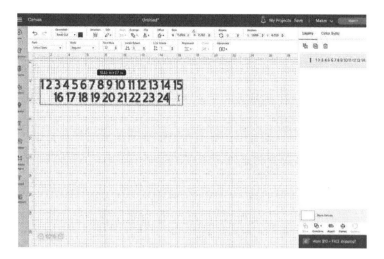

Click on font and select 'Ariel black'. This font is nice and thick and it doesn't tear easily. It's not flimsy and makes it easy to glue onto other materials.

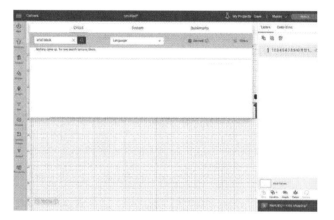

Resize the numbers. Since the entire numbers are still grouped, go to the top menu and type in 2 inches in height. This will change each number to be 2 inches in height automatically.

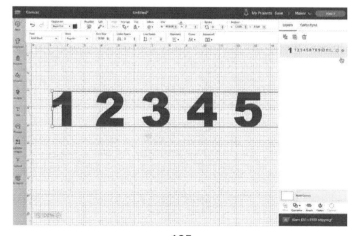

On the right-hand side of the layer panel, there is an error message displayed saying that the numbers are too large and will go off from the cutting mat when the cutting process starts. This is because the entire numbers are still attached. Click 'ungroup' so that the numbers will be cut individually.

Click 'Make It'.

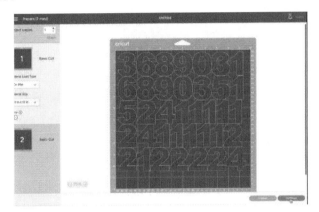

Set your materials and tools.

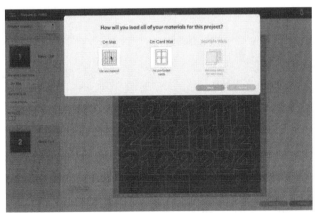

Place the cardstock on a mat and put it into the machine to cut. After cutting, remove the numbers from the mat and weed them.

Take the brown paper bags and paste the stickers on each bag. just to add a flair to it.

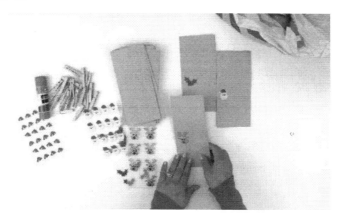

Grab the numbers, apply glue at the back of the numbers, and stick them in the center front of each brown bag.

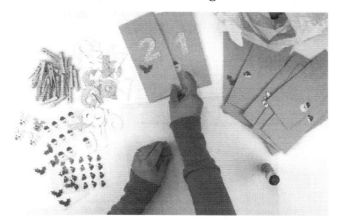

Add an advent gift in each pay and use a peg to seal off each bag.

Your Advent calendar is ready!

Halloween Masks

Materials Needed

- o Cricut machine
- o Cricut strong grip mat
- o Craft form (2mm)- purple, yellow, green, and multi-colors.
- o Craft glue (Kalau)
- o Needle tip bottle for glue
- o Weeding tool
- o Washi tape/masking tape/painter's tape.

Instructions

Open the design space and tap on 'projects.' Type 'masks' in the search box and select a design. Click 'continue' to bring it into the design space canvas.

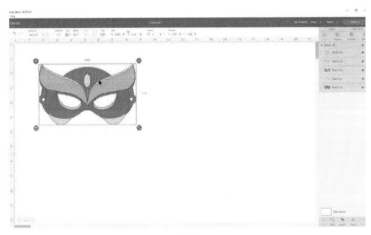

Resize the mask to 7 inches wide and click 'Make It'. Set your materials to 'craft foam' and tools to 'knife blades' and 'deep point blades.' Place the craft foam on a Cricut strong grip mat and secure the four sides with washi tape, masking tape, or painter's tape.

Put it in the Cricut machine to cut. Cut different layers of the Mask.

Flip the back of the first layer and apply glue around it.

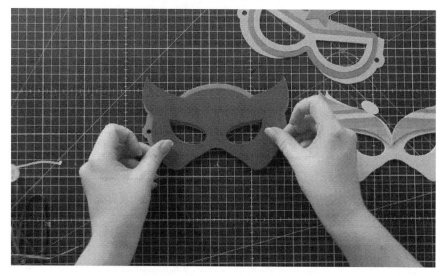

Align it along the bottom and adhere it. Apply glue to another layer and affix it until all layers are assembled. Let the mask dry. Cut an elastic rope and thread it through both holes on the sides of the ear. Your mask is now ready!

Easter Basket Tags

Materials Needed

- o Cricut machine
- o Cricut mat
- o Bunny ornaments
- o Vinyl
- o Watercolors
- o Ribbons
- o Jewish wines
- o Transfer tape
- o Scraper
- o Mod podge

Instructions

Open the design space and click on 'new project'. Click on the text icon and type the name: Kingsley. Noella, Addison.

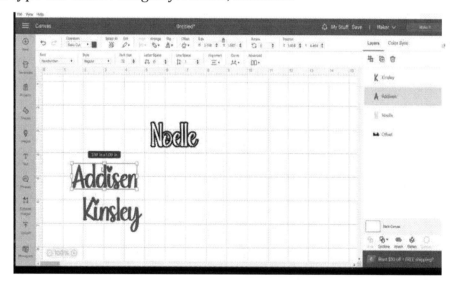

Change the font by clicking on font and selecting a script font.

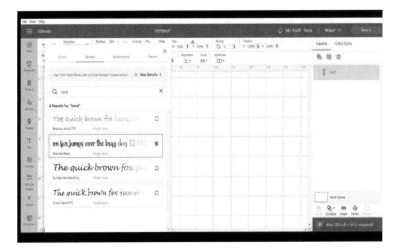

Resize the name by measuring the blanks.

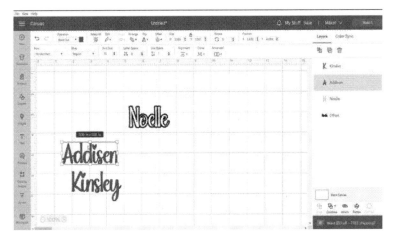

Click 'Make It'. Preview the mat screen to ensure everything sits well on the mat and click 'continue.' Set your material to regular vinyl and set the tools.

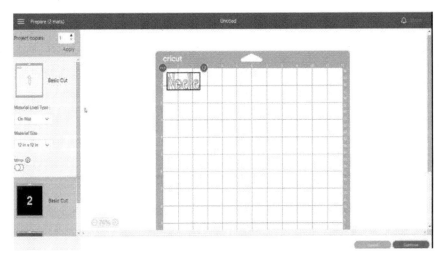

Place your vinyl on the mat and insert it in the Cricut machine to cut.

Peel off the design from the mat and weed out the excess vinyl.

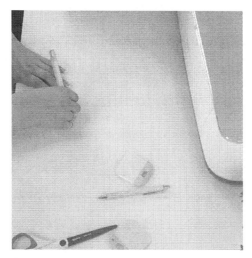

Cut enough transfer tape to cover the design. Place it on top of your design and use a scraper to press it down until the design sticks to the transfer tape. Gently peel back the transfer tape.

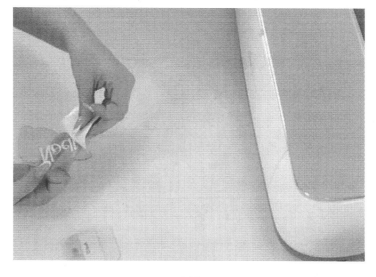

Place the transfer tape with the vinyl on it on the bunny ornament. Use a scraper to press it down removing all bubbles. Peel back the transfer tape.

Repeat this step for the other names. Apply a layer of Mod Podge on the surface of your design and allow it to dry. Cut small lengths of ribbon and thread onto the bunny blanks.

Thanksgiving Table Centerpieces

Materials Needed

- o Cricut machine
- o Cricut standard grip mat
- o Cricut easy press
- o Wedding tool
- o Scraper
- o Heat transfer vinyl
- o Table cloth

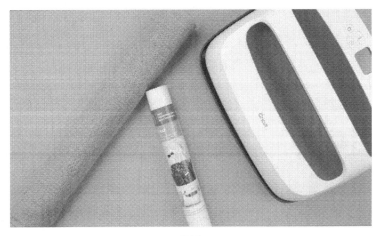

Instructions

Open the design space and click on 'new project'. Click on the text icon and type 'Thankful'. Go to fonts on the top menu and select a script font. Adjust the spacing between the letters to touch each other by clicking on the letter spacing icon. If the letters are still not touching each other or connected, click 'Ungroup' to move the letters manually. Resize the text by measuring the space where you want to place it. Make it about 7 inches wide by 4 inches high. Change the text color to white and then click 'weld' so that Cricut will cut it as one piece.

Click 'Make It'. Preview the mat screen and ensure that the mirror icon is turned on.

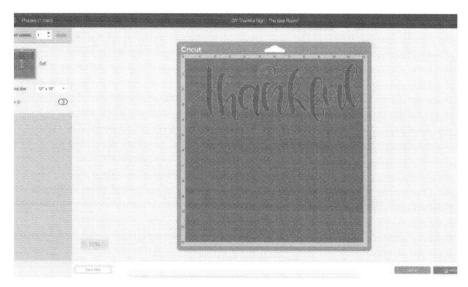

Click 'continue'. Set your material- heat transfer vinyl and tool.

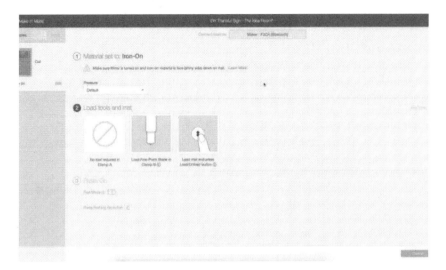

Position the heat transfer vinyl on a mat with the shiny side facing downward, then insert it into the Cricut machine for cutting.

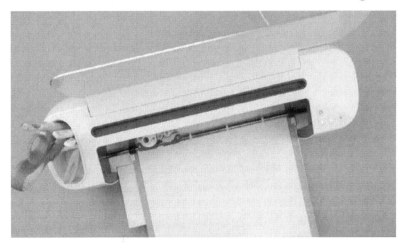

After cutting, peel off the vinyl from the mat and weed your design.

Set the Cricut easy press to a temperature of 220°. Spread the tablecloth and preheat the spot you want to place the design.

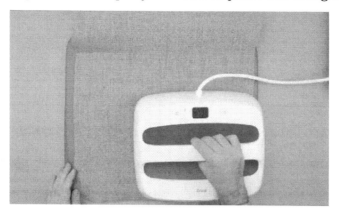

Position the vinyl on the tablecloth and place the easy press on the design for 30 seconds.

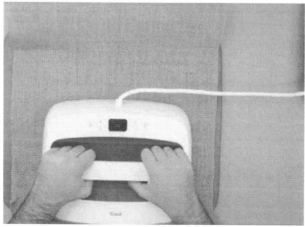

Leave it to cool, then remove the plastic.

Chapter 7

Kids' Crafts

DIY Play Masks

Materials Needed

- o Cricut machine
- o Cricut mat
- o Cardstock
- o Wedding tool
- o Popsicle sticks
- o Craft glue
- o Glue gun

Instructions

Open the design space and type - animal masks in the search bar of Cricut Access

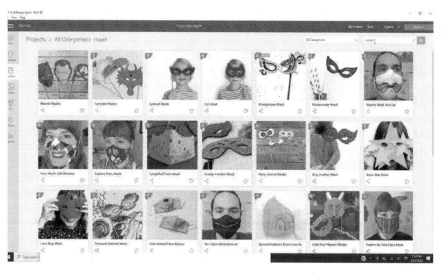

Select the desired option. It will display all the necessary components for the project along with assembly instructions. You can also print this for easy reference during assembly.

Click 'Customize it' if you still want to make some changes and adjustments or click 'Make it'. I don't need to make any adjustments so click 'make it'.

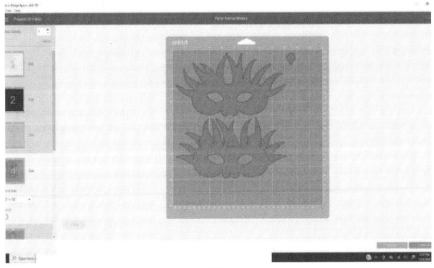

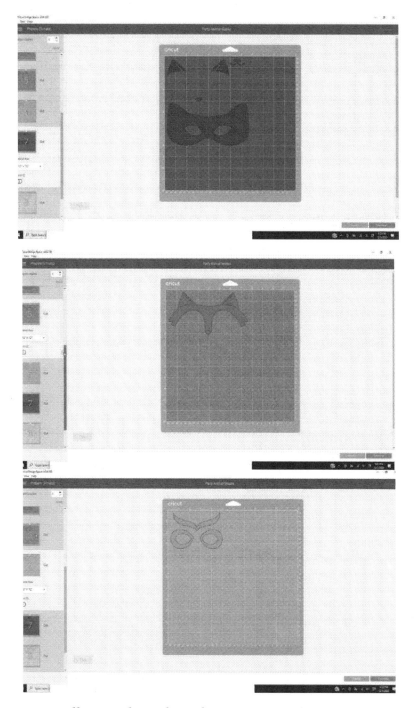

Cricut access tells you the color of paper to use but you can make it in any color of your choice. Set your material- Cardstock and tools. Place the cardstock on a mat and insert it in the Cricut machine for cutting. Remove your design from the mat and weed out the excess cardstock. Apply glue at the back of the second layer and stick it on the top of the first layer.

Flip the mask, add glue to one end of a popsicle stick and place it on the right-hand side.

Assemble the other mask the same way.

Personalized Lunchbox Notes

Materials Needed

- o Cricut machine (marker or explorer)
- o Cricut light grip cutting mat
- o Card stocks

o   Color printer.

Instructions

Open the design space, go to 'projects,' and type on the search for kindness, positivity, happiness and affirmations. Select the ones you want and click on 'add to canvas.'

Add color to the notes and resize them to fit into the lunchbox. Go to the top menu and change the project from basic cut to 'print and cut'.

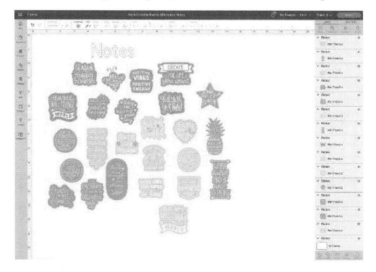

Tap "Make It". follow the on-screen instructions to connect your device and choose the cutting material - cardstock. Put it into the colored printer to print the notes. Place your printed material on the cutting mat with the printed side facing upward. Put it in the Cricut machine to cut.

After cutting, gently remove the notes from the mat.

Place the notes in your child's lunchbox every morning.

Paper Bag Puppets

- o Cricut machine

- o Cricut light grip mat

- o Paper lunch bags- Green or brown

- o Craft glue

Instructions

Go to Google and type 'paper front Puppet'. Select the one you want and download the PNG file. Upload the PNG file of the frog puppet to Cricut Design Space and tap on "simple".

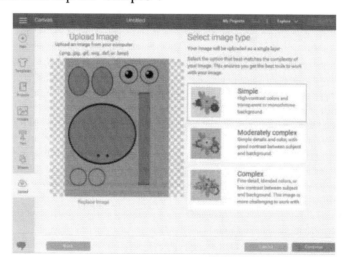

Zoom out if necessary, click on the white background to eliminate it, and save it as "print then cut."

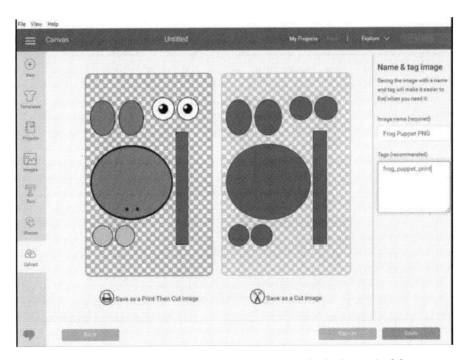

Tap on the uploaded frog puppet template and click on 'add to canvas'. Adjust the size of the entire image group and ensure an eye is approximately 1.5 inches wide.

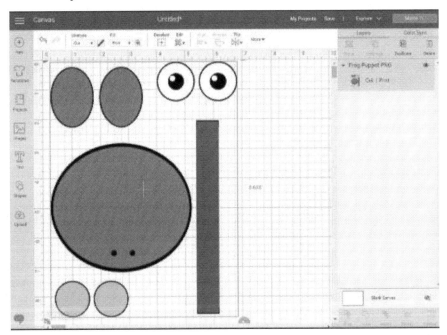

Tap on "Make It." Follow the on-screen instructions to print it before laying it on a mat and into the Cricut machine. Remember to leave the bleed on.

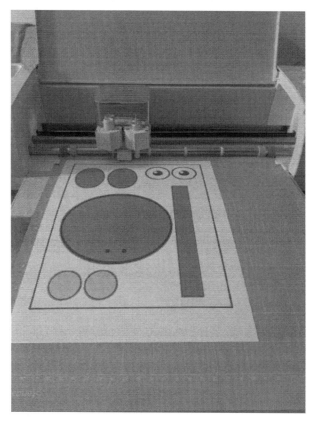

Once the cutting is complete, carefully detach the pieces from the mat. Now, the components are set for assembly.

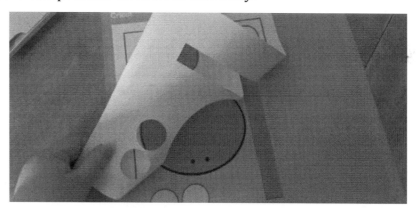

Assemble the parts with glue. Apply glue at the back of the large circle, which will serve as the frog's head and place it at the bottom of the bag.

Next, attach the eyeballs to the green ovals that are glued to the top of the head. Apply glue at the back of the tiny pink circles for the cheeks and stick them. Curl the red strip around a pencil to create the tongue, then glue it beneath the head's base.

Slide your hand into the bag and let your frog go ribbit.

Craft Stick Art Projects

Materials Needed

- o Cricut machine
- o Cricut strong grip mat

- o Craft Foam
- o Craft Glue
- o Oval wood blanks

Instructions

Open the design space and click on templates. Select some images of animals and dinosaurs you want then click customize.

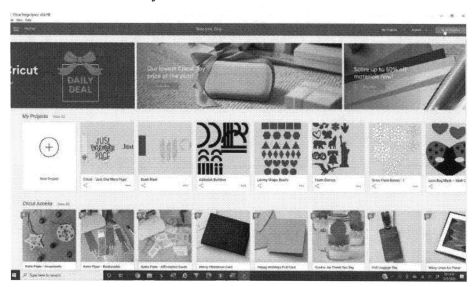

Resize the images and arrange them to fit into one mat and Click 'Make It'. Tap continue on the mat preview screen.

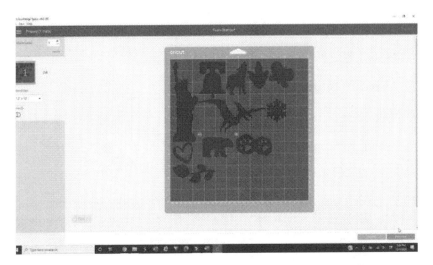

Place the craft form on a strong grip mat and put it into the Cricut to cut.

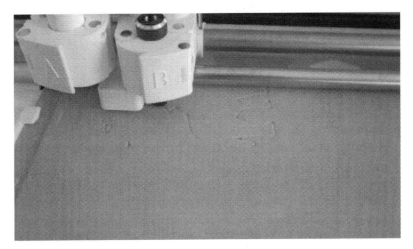

After cutting, remove your design from the mat gently.

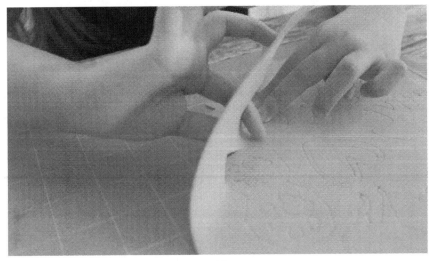

Flip the cut image and apply some glue to it.

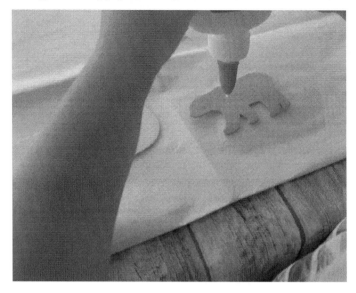

Place it on the oval wood blanks and press down to stick properly.

Repeat this same step for the other cut images. The wood image stamp is ready.

Chapter 8

Organization and Labels

Customized Magazine Holders

Materials Needed

- o Cricut machine
- o Scissors
- o Paint
- o Smart label writable paper
- o Paintbrush
- o Writing stylus

Instructions

Paint your magazine holder in the chosen color and allow them to dry thoroughly. It might be necessary to administer two layers. During the drying process, launch the Cricut Design Space application and initiate a fresh project. Access the "Image" library and locate the image #M7D7D5E8. Click on this image and incorporate it into your project canvas. Remember, image codes are case-sensitive.

During image selection, go to the "Action" menu and click on "Hide Contour." Conceal the inner line of the image to prevent the machine from cutting along this specific line.

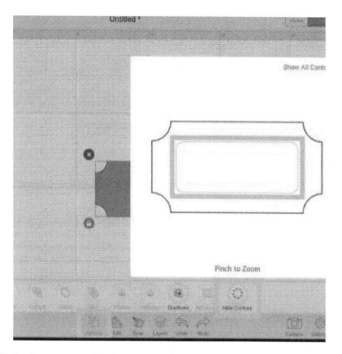

Resize the label to match the front of the magazine holder accurately. Measure if needed to ensure precision. The label was adjusted to 3" wide using the "Edit" menu.

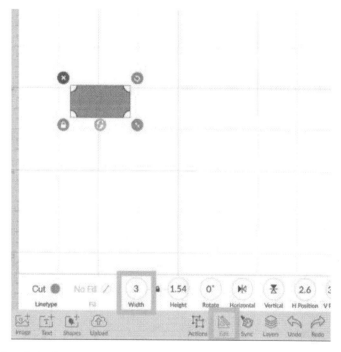

Duplicate the label twice or as required for your project by accessing the "Action" menu.

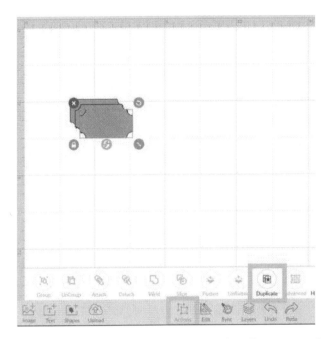

Click on the "Text library and pick a font with a "Writing Style," such as Cricut Sans. After selecting the font, input your initial label name. Highlight the label text and modify the font style to "writing" using the options available in the "Edit" menu.

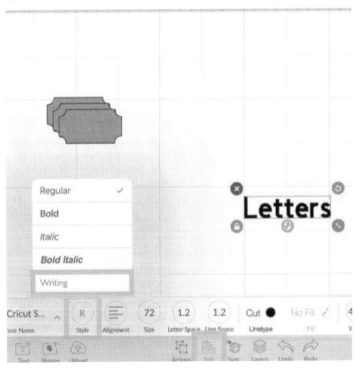

Adjust your label text to suit the label shape. In this case, adjust to a width of 2.5" using the options in the "Edit" menu.

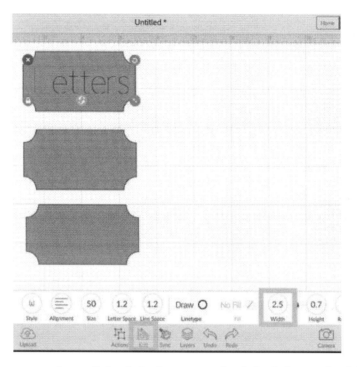

For precise centering of the label text on the label shape, highlight both the text and one label. In the "Edit" menu, choose "Align" and from there, you can center the elements accurately.

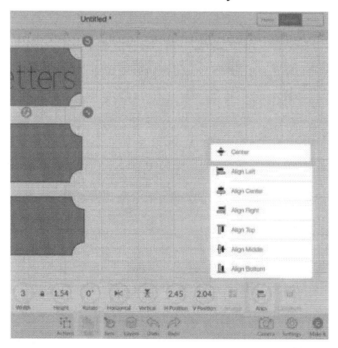

After aligning and selecting both the label and text, access the "Actions" menu and click "Attach".

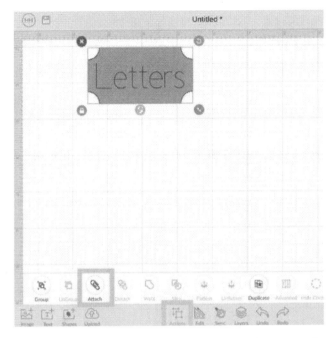

This secures the placement of your written label name. Repeat the last three steps for the remaining labels.

Select "Make It" and specify the material load type. When working with a Smart Label, choose "Without Mat" to ensure proper handling of the material.

Select 'continue' in the mat preview screen. Choose your material setting- "Smart Label Writable Paper".

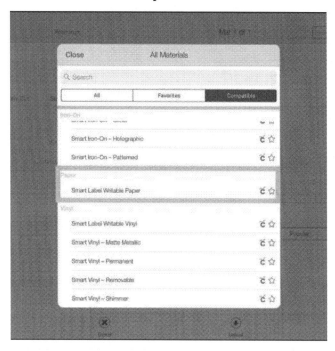

Adhere to the on-screen guidance, place your pen into the Cricut machine, and ensure your blade is set. When prompted, put your material into the machine.

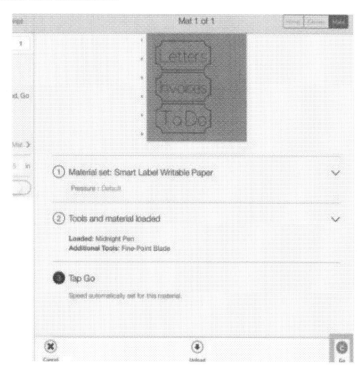

After cutting, remove your project and trim any excess material to save for future projects.

Detach your Smart Labels from the liner sheet and affix them to the front of the magazine holder.

Personalized File Folders

Materials Needed

- o Cricut machine
- o Cricut mat
- o Cardstock

- o Clear little tabs

- o Hanging folders

Instructions

Measure your little file tab holders. For this project we will use 2 inches by 0.5 inches. Open design space, choose a shape- square. Resize it to 2 inches by 0.5 inch. Here at the operation, it says basic cut so the Cricut machine is going to cut this basic square out. Change the color to white because it will be cut out of a white card stock with black text written on it for the file labels.

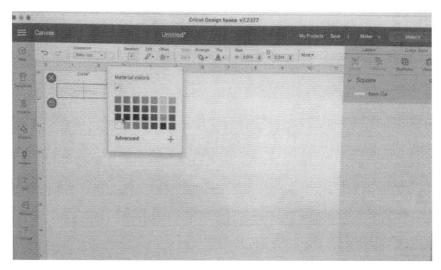

Click on the text and select a font- 'dear John.' Make the labels in caps. Type 'PHOTO'. Click on the text and shrink it down to where you want to put it- inside the square. The 'photo' defaults to 'basic cut'. I want it to be written by Cricut. Choose a pen type- black. Use the fine point 0.4mm in black.

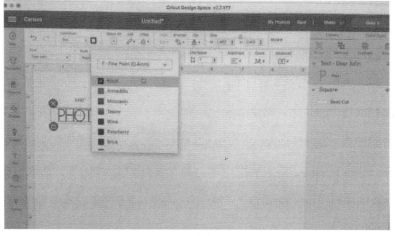

Now Cricut is going to cut the white square and use the ink pen to write on your file tab the text that you prefer.

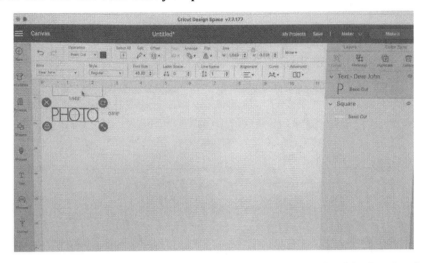

You can see that the 'h' and the 'o' are a bit closer, highlight the letters and make the letter spacing a little bit apart. Select everything, click 'align', and then tap 'center horizontally and vertically.'

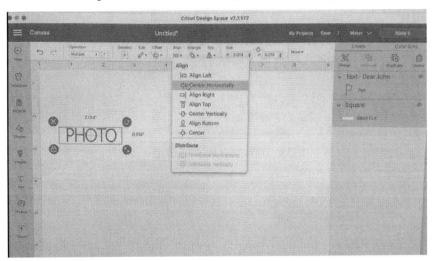

To do the remaining labels, highlight everything and click 'duplicate'. Tap on the duplicate and change the 'PHOTO' to read 'COPY'. This will be for the copy paper. Now, it has defaulted back to the basic cut. Choose a pen to underdraw and select pen type 0.4 mm in black. Highlight the copy and the square click align and then tap on center horizontally and vertically. Repeat these same steps for the next label after you click duplicate. Highlight all the labels and click 'attach'. This will tell Cricut to write on the actual square that you have chosen for your file labels. Click 'Make It'.

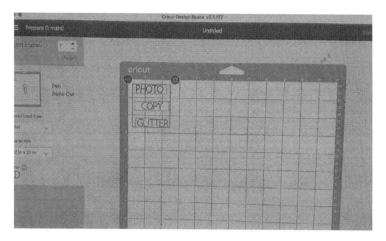

Click 'continue' in the mat review screen. Set your base material to heavy cardstock and set your tools -the black pen in clamp A and the fine point blade in clamp B.

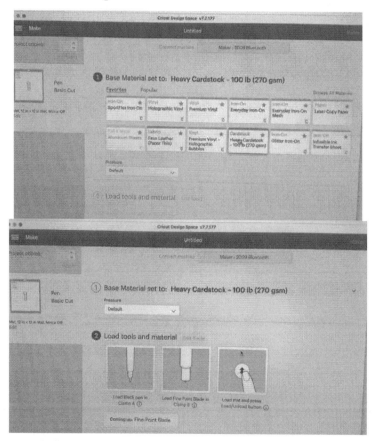

Place the cardstock on a mat and put it in the Cricut machine to cut and write.

After cutting, bend your mat a little bit and peel off the cardstock. Take the clear little tabs, put the photo label in it and press down to close.

Attach it to the hanging tab folder.

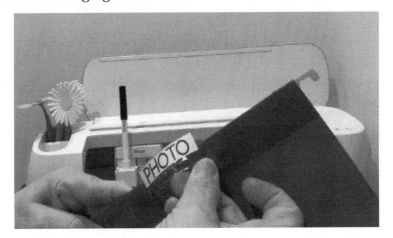

The finished look of the project.

Kitchen Conversion Charts

Cabinet Decals

Materials Needed

o Cricut machine

o Cricut mat

- o Wedding tool
- o Scraper
- o Transfer tape
- o Regular vinyl
- o Lightboard
- o Vinyl cutting board

Instructions

Go to Google and type 'kitchen conversion chart templates'. Select one, download it, and save it on your device. Take away all the background and make all the white spaces to be transparent. Click apply and continue.

Select the image and upload it.

173

Click to add it to your canvas. Measure the space on the cabinet you want to place it in. In this case 10 inches.

Go back to the design space and resize the image to 10 inches in height and 8 inches in width.

Click 'Make It'. If everything looks good on the mat preview screen, tap continue.

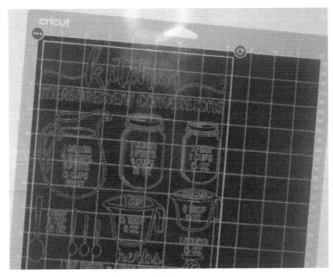

Set your materials- regular vinyl and tools.

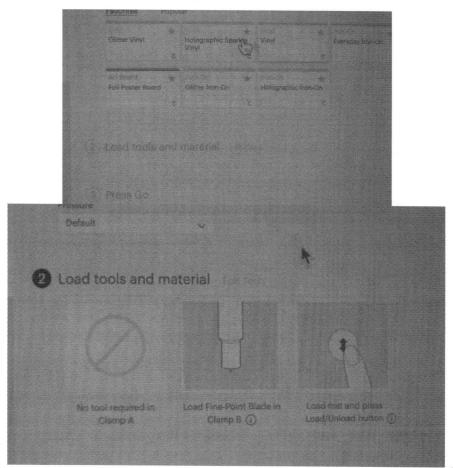

Place the vinyl on the mat and put it in the Cricut to cut.

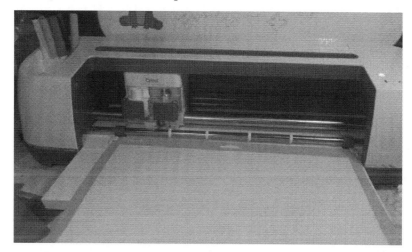

Place the vinyl on the light board and weed the design.

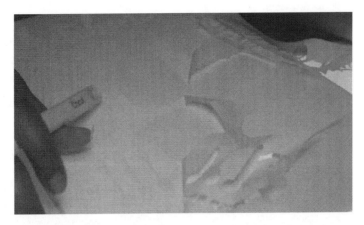

Cut out transfer tape the same size as the design. Place it over the vinyl and use the scraper to press it down, removing all bubbles. Peel off your design.

Place the vinyl on the cabinet and press down with the scraper.

Pull off the transfer leaving your design on the cabinet.

The final look of the project.

Customized Drawer Dividers

Materials Needed

- o Cricut machine
- o Cricut blue light grip mat
- o Cardstock (80lb)
- o Tacky glue
- o Wedding tool.

Instructions

Go to Google and type 'drawer divider'. Select one, download it, and save it on your device. Launch the Cricut Design Space and select the 'upload' option. Browse to search and select the Drawer divider svg file. Tap then click add to canvas.

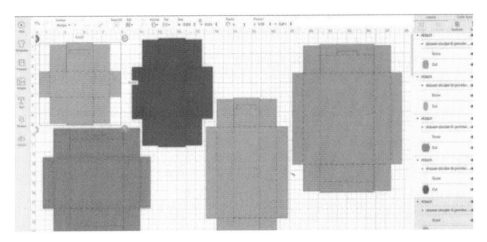

Go to the operation menu to change the score line layer from "Cut" to "Score". Next, highlight both the core layer and the cut layer and click "Attach" to ensure the divider is properly scored. Tap 'Make It'. Ensure that the design is set as both score and cut at the left-hand side of the layer panel. Tap' continue'.

Set your materials- 80lb cardstock and tools- deep point blade and scoring stylus. Also, set the pressure to 'more'. Place the cardstock on a light grip mat and put it in the machine to cut. After cutting, remove the cardstock from the mat by flipping the mat over and peeling the mat away from the cardstock.

This will prevent the design from curling up and ripping the cardstock. Position your paper with the desired inside surface facing upward.

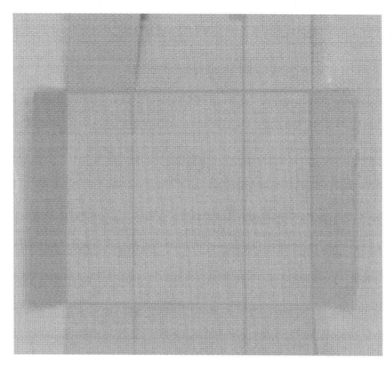

Fold your drawer divider following the fold lines depicted in the provided photo.

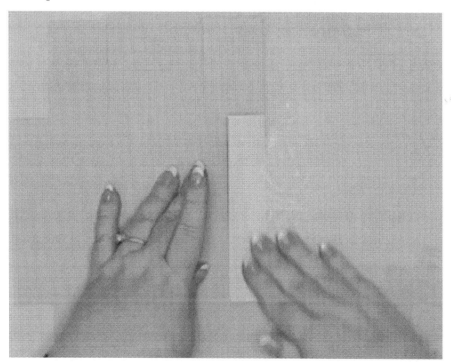

Do a total of 10 folds, directing each one inward to start the folding process. Turn your paper to the opposite side and fold in the four flaps in the opposite direction, as illustrated in the photo below.

179

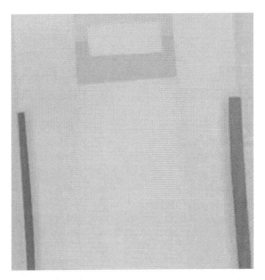

Return your folded paper to its initial state and start gluing the sides. Apply glue to two sets of side wings simultaneously, as demonstrated in the provided example. If uncertain about which side to apply glue, consider initially folding the box to observe the assembly. Ensure that the wings are positioned on the exterior of the box, not the interior.

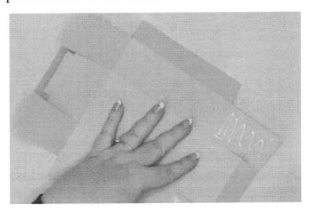

After applying adhesive to the side wings, firmly press them down and give the glue a moment to stick (approximately 30 seconds).

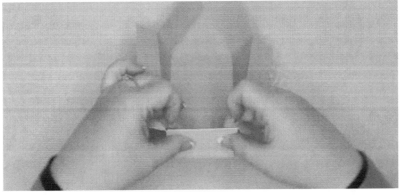

Flip the drawer divider box and attach glue to the remaining side wings.

Secure the drawer divider by gluing down all four side flaps to reinforce the upper edges and enhance its strength.

Chapter 9

Tech Accessories

DIY Cord Protectors

Materials Needed

- o Cricut machine.
- o Cricut mat
- o Faux leather
- o Snap buttons (studs, sockets and caps)
- o Poking tool
- o Cables

Instructions

Open the design space and click on a new canvas. Go to shapes and select a shape.

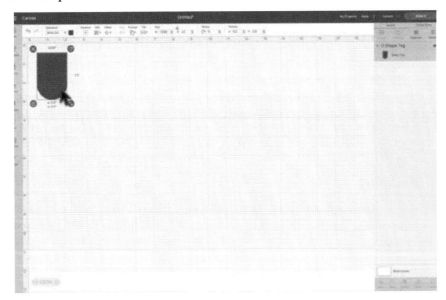

Click on shapes again and select a circle.

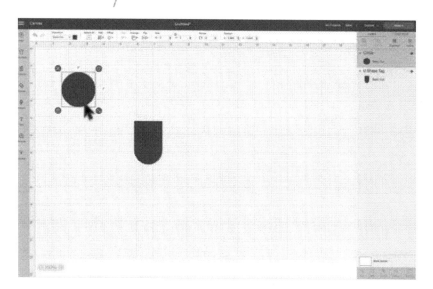

This is for the holes. Resize the circle to 0.05, change the color and place the small circle on the first shape.

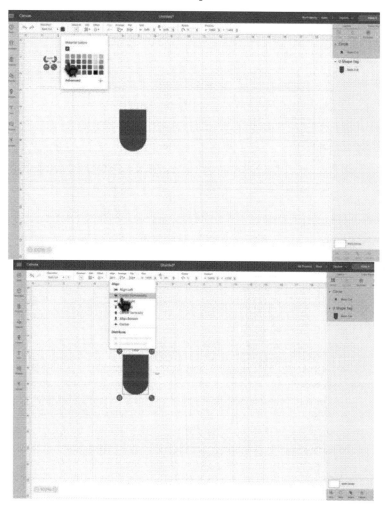

183

This is where the snap buttons will be placed. Delete the circle. Select all, click 'align' and then 'center horizontally'. Tap 'slice'.

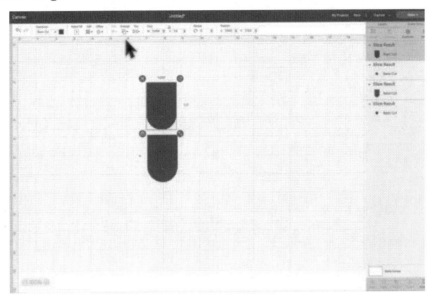

While the shape is still selected, click 'duplicate'. Align the two vertically. While the other shape is still selected, click flip and then tap on flip vertically to align them together. Select the two shapes, check 'align', and then tap 'center horizontally' and while they are still selected tap on 'weld'.

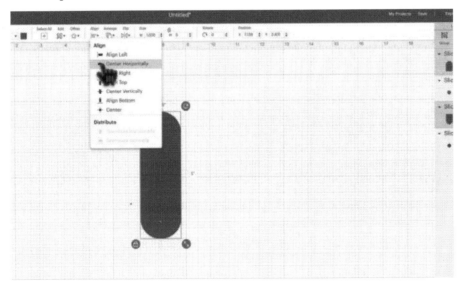

Delete the tiny circle and change the height to 0.4 inches. Set it aside. Click on 'images', and on the search bar type 'bunny'.

Select one and click 'add to canvas'.

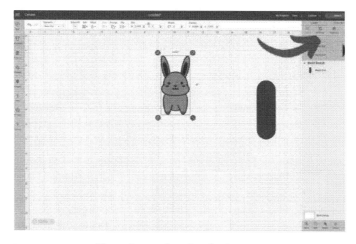

While the image is still selected, cluck 'ungroup.' Separate the two images. Leave the silhouette and hide the other image for now.

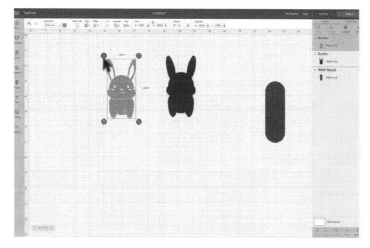

Select the eye icon in the layer To create holes on the snap button, go to shapes select a circle and change the size to 0.05 inches. Change the color and drag the circle to where you want the snap button to be placed. Select the image click 'align', then tap 'center horizontally' and click 'slice'. Make another hole for the snap button. Drag and place it where you want the snap button to be.

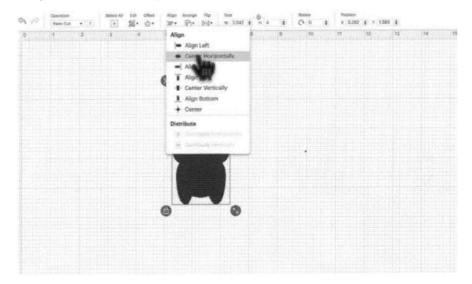

This part will be folded in half. If your cable is thick and you prefer not to wrap it too tightly in this cable holder, adjust the height to 5 inches or more. Select all, click 'align', choose 'center horizontally', and then click 'slice'. Remove all the small circles from the holes, leaving only one. To create another cable holder, go to images, select a bear, and click 'add to canvas.'

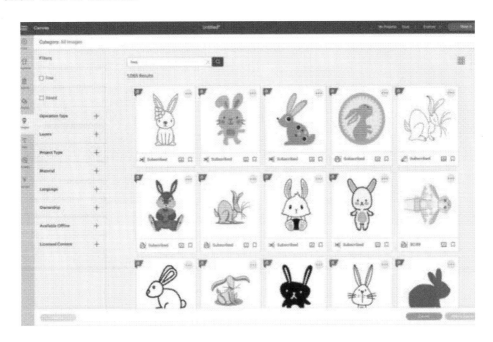

Repeat the steps like I did with the bunny.

Make the cable holders be of two colors so that they can all be on one mat and then click 'Make It'.

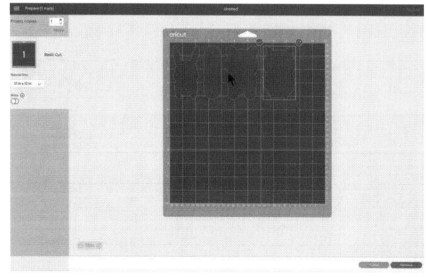

I'll use two different colors of faux leather, so I'll separate them and place each on the mat accordingly. Then, I'll click 'continue'. Set the material to full leather paper thin and adjust the pressure to 'more.'

Place the leather on the mat, use painter's tape to hold it down, and place it in the Cricut to cut.

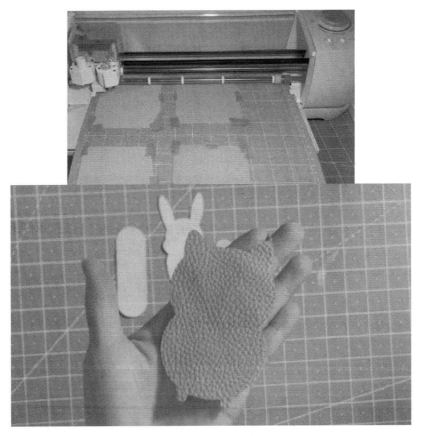

Use the tool to poke it and fix the snap buttons. These are what we need for the snap button- studs, sockets and caps.

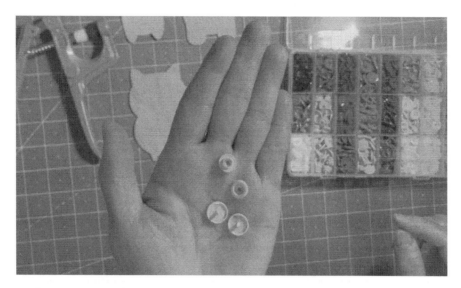

Insert the cap into the hole and grab the tool. The flat side or the cap of the snap button goes to this side of the tool.

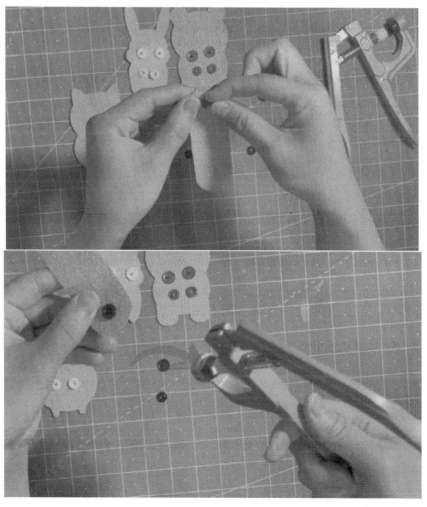

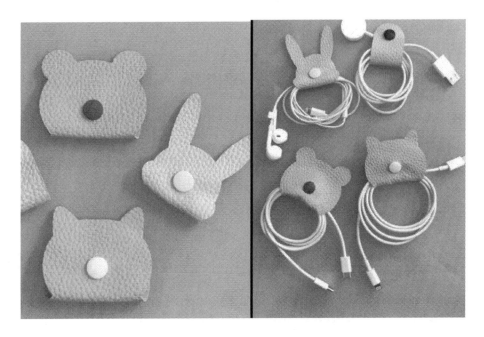

Customized Laptop Sleeves

Materials Needed

- Purpose laptop decal design or an empty laptop template is available in the free library under the 'Stickers' section.

- Measuring tape

- Clear Printable Vinyl Sheets Inkjet

- Printer or Laser Printer,

- Cricut Maker, or a Cricut Explore Air 2

- Cricut Light Grip Mat

- Painter's Tape (or another light-adhesive tape)

- Cricut scraper.

- Paper Trimmer

Keep in mind that white won't be printed and will appear transparent. Choose the WHITE Printable Vinyl if you want to retain the white aspect or if you're using a dark-colored laptop. Select one of the free designs labeled "dark" in the file name to avoid a white border.

Instructions

Tap to open the library of creative resources. Once you get to 'Printable Art and Stickers,' continue scrolling down. Our desire is 'Purpose Laptop Skin.' To download, click the provided link. To access options, double-click or click and hold, then select "Save to downloads." Get the zip file open. Select 'New Canvas' when Cricut Design Space opens on your desktop. From the toolbar on the left side of the website, select the Upload option. Select Browse. Your computer should now be able to access your files.

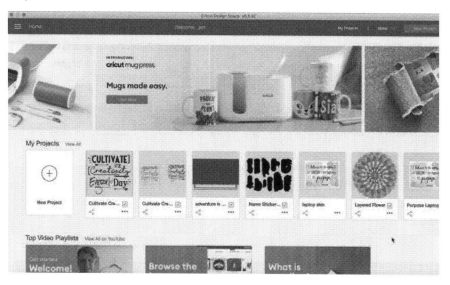

Choose either the 'Purpose Laptop Skin' PNG design or the 'Empty Laptop Skin' PNG design. Select 'Complex' when prompted, and then tap 'Continue'. Bypass the Clean-up page, and save the file as a 'Print then Cut'.

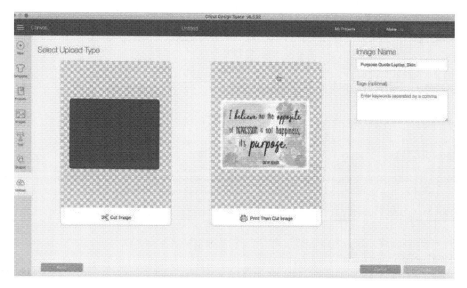

Add it to your Uploaded Images, select it and tap "Insert Images" in the bottom right corner to see it on your canvas.

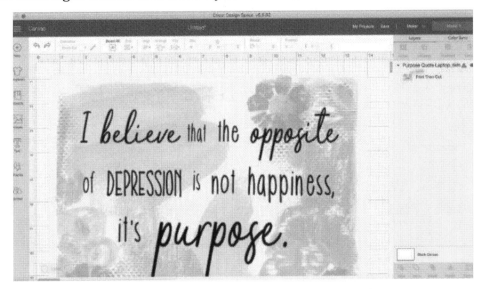

Adjust the size using the options in the top toolbar. If you prefer a size smaller than 6.75" x 9.25," measure the front top of the laptop using a ruler and make the necessary adjustments. Optionally, unlock the lock icon above Size in the top toolbar to modify constraints by entering your desired height and width.

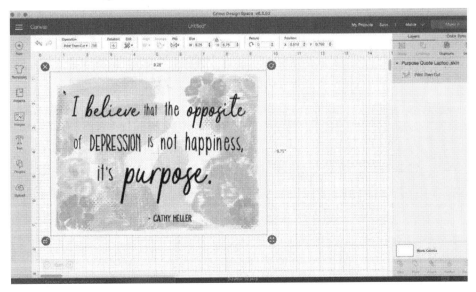

Choose the Text icon in the side toolbar to open the Text Panel. Enter your desired text, position it on the mat as needed, and make font and size adjustments according to your preferences.

When using a cursive font, you can separate the letters, reposition them, and weld them together if you're cutting. However, for print and cut, this becomes unnecessary as we flatten the design. After arranging everything to your preference, select all the text and click 'Attach'. Then, Select All, click on 'Align', and tap 'Center', and then click 'Flatten'. Remember that this action is reversible, but it essentially instructs your machine to treat it as a unified print and cut.

Ensure to save your project, then click "Make it!" to proceed with the mat preview screen.

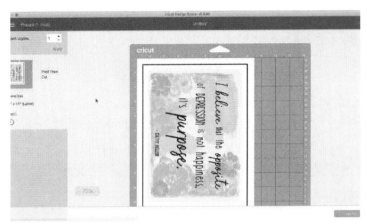

Insert your Printable Vinyl into the printer. On your display, locate the print box and deactivate the bleed option.

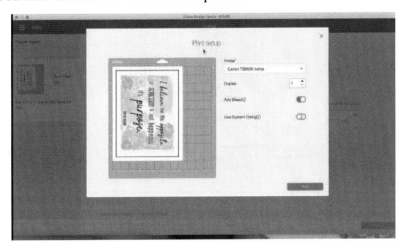

If you prefer using your printer's dialog box, activate the System Dialog*. Press the Print button. The majority of printable vinyl inherently possesses water resistance or waterproof properties. The ink permeates the vinyl, providing a certain level of protection against regular wear and tear. Apply a laminate to add a clear overlay and provide a protective layer to your design.

Position your printed image on the Light Grip Cutting Mat following the Mat Preview Page guide. Apply firm pressure or use a brayer to secure it in place.

Select Premium Vinyl in the material settings and place the vinyl on your mat.

Obey the instructions on your machine: place the fine point blade and the press 'Go' button.

195

After it's done, make sure the vinyl is cut thoroughly, and then remove your mat.

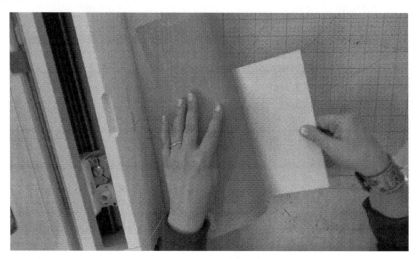

Cut out the black lines using a small page trimmer.

Alternatively, you may simply remove the extra vinyl by pulling it off the backing paper.

Ensure your surface is clean and lint-free. Use an alcohol-based wipe to clean the surface. Allow it to dry before proceeding to apply your laptop sleeve. Place your design in the middle of the laptop cover. Put a piece of tape on the side of your design that has been trimmed. Thus, a "hinge" is created.

Raise the top of the vinyl sheet with the printing and fold the backing paper back.

Smooth down the design using the scraper to remove all air bubbles.

Vinyl Decals for Gaming Consoles

Materials Needed

- o Cricut machine
- o Cricut mat
- o Inkjet printer
- o Printable vinyl
- o Transparent permanent vinyl
- o Paper trimmer
- o Scraper
- o Cardstock

Instructions

Open a new canvas in the design space and go to the image library. Click on images and then on image sets.

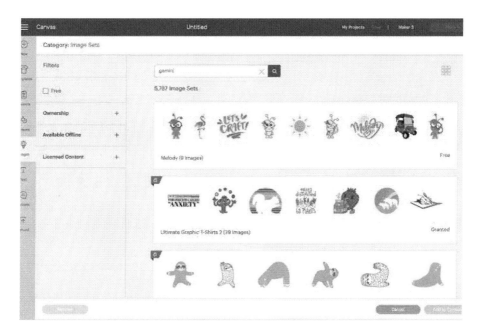

Click on this image set and select the multi-colored image that you like.

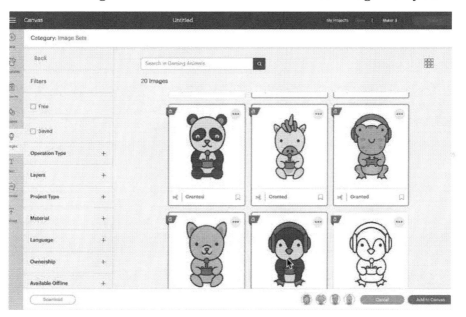

Add them to the canvas.

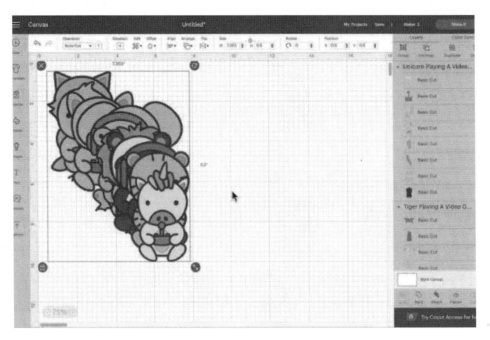

They all come packed together. Click outside the bounding box and then you can click each one individually to resize and rotate. Separate them from each other, resize them to about the same size, and rearrange them.

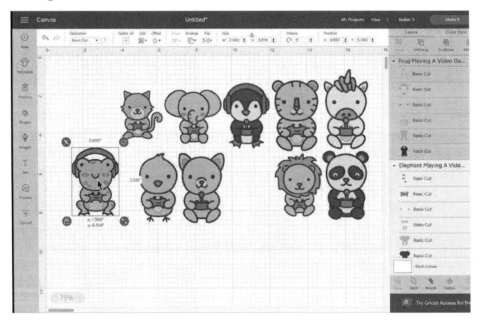

Most of the images need an offset, to create a solid background for small details like this little frog and his headphone. Select the front and click on the offset feature on the background layer. Use 0.1 offsets for stickers. You can use the slider but it is easier to type a size. Look at the image to preview the amount of offset for the sticker before you click 'apply'.

Ensure that the offset is basic cut and the color is white. That way you won't waste ink and it's easier to see when you arrange the stickers on the templates. In the layer panel, you can see it's a separate layer. If the offset isn't solid, select the offset and click contour, close the contour screen to see the result. In the layer panel, hold down the shift button select the frog and its offset, and click flatten. Cricut will cut the offset line of my printed sticker.

Do the same for the cat and the chicken. Ensure you flatten out all of the images before continuing to the next step. The maximum printable area for print and then cut is 6.75 inches by 9.25 inches. Create a template to get the most out of the material by arranging the stickers within that area. Insert a square from the shape panel, resize it to the maximum printable area, change it to a light gray color, and then right-click send to back.

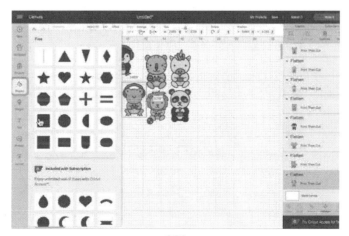

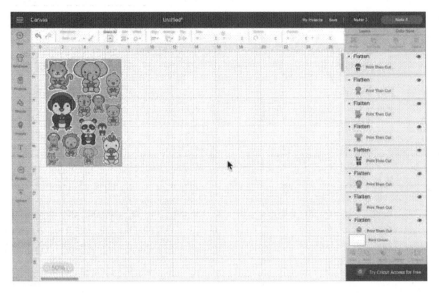

This will allow you to see the white border of the sticker. Resize and arrange all the sticker images on this sheet. Remember the goal is to get the most out of stickers out of my sheet. You can add more images from the image library or duplicate or resize some of your favorites. Once your page is full, go to the gray rectangle template and hide or delete the template using the layer panels. Select all and click 'attach'. This will preserve the placement of the images on the printed page. Next, save your project and click ' Make It'.

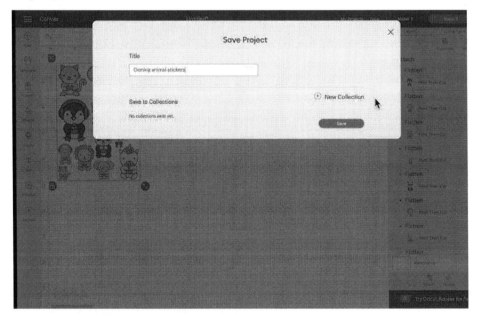

In the prepare screen, you will see how your sticker will print out, note the orientation.

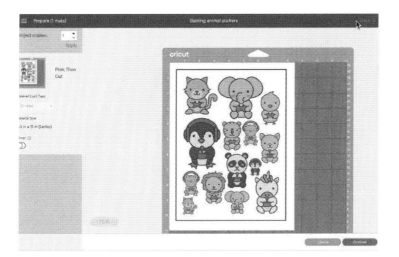

Place the paper up in the top left-hand corner of the mat click continue and then send it to the printer.

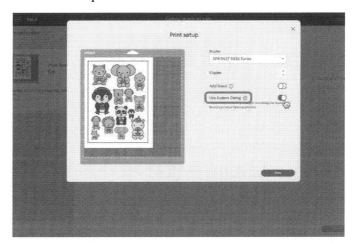

Use the system dialog box to improve the print quality. Increase the print quality to the best

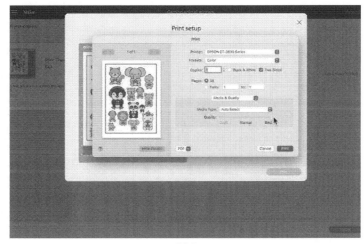

Ensure you have printable vinyl placed correctly in the printer then click print.

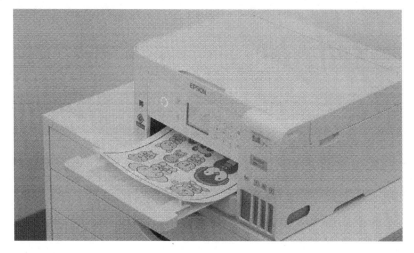

Once the sheet is printed, set it aside to dry to prevent smudges. To make your stickers water-resistant, cover them before you cut them out with transparent permanent vinyl. To do this, measure and cut a piece to fit inside the black outline box.

Ensure you don't cover or smudge ink on the box because that is what Cricut uses to orient itself for the cut. To achieve neat, straight lines, use a paper trimmer.

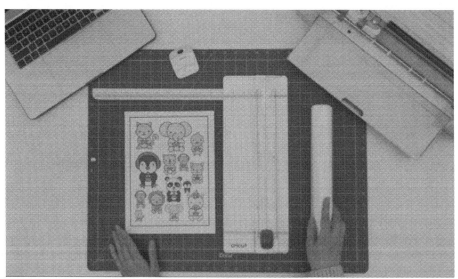

Make sure that the transparent permanent vinyl fits within the black rectangle without touching it. Peel the top inch of the transparent vinyl backer away and crease it down. Place the exposed part flat onto your sticker paper.

Do not cover the rectangle. Use your scraper or your hand to roll the backer away while sticking the vinyl down.

Avoid shifting the transparent vinyl onto your black rectangle. Once that is ready, place the printed page on the top left-hand corner of the mat and smooth it with a brayer to ensure it's solidly placed.

Go back to design space select the material - transparent vinyl and set it to deep cutting. Click browse all materials and select cardstock.

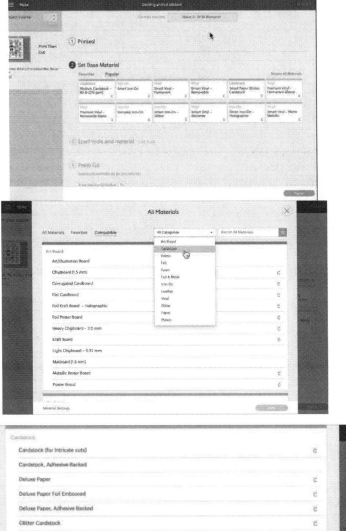

Put the mat into the machine to cut.

After cutting, check if the stickers are cut as desired. If not, press the go button for another pass. Once it is done, remove the sheet or individual stickers from the mat by flipping over the mat and parking it away from your project.

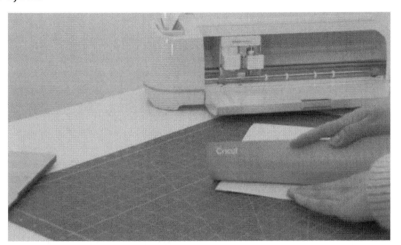

Personalized Mouse Pads

Materials Needed

- o Cricut machine
- o Cricut Easypress
- o Sublimation Mouse pad
- o Heat transfer tape
- o Infusible ink sheets

- Butcher paper

- Cardstock

- Easy press mat

- Watercolor pattern

- Washi tape

- Tweezers

Instructions

Open a new canvas on design space. Click on the text and type 'Once you become fearless life becomes limitless.' Select two different fonts- a script don't for 'fearless & Limitless and a thick-block font for the others. Adjust the spacings between the letters especially the script fonts to connect and also adjust the line spacings.

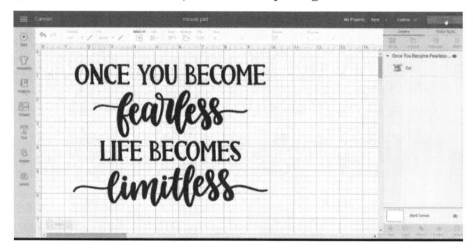

Click 'Make It' and mirror your cut.

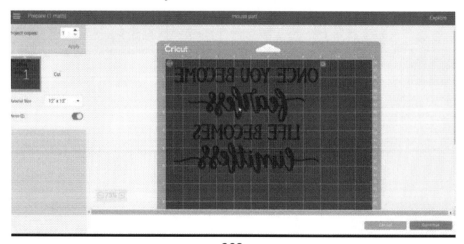

Center the design. The mouse pad is about 9.25 inches wide and 7.75 inches high. Click 'continue'. Set the material to an infusible ink sheet.

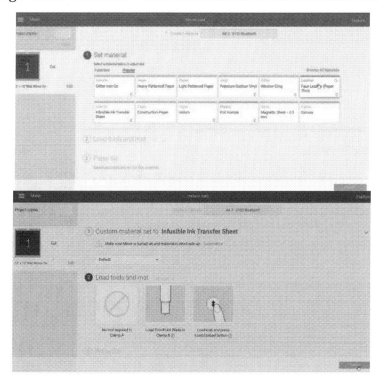

Place the Infusible Ink sheet with the liner facing down on the mat, ensuring the ink side is facing up. Mirror your cut before placing it in the cutting machine. Peel the mat back from the Infusible Ink sheet once the cutting is complete. Trim the sheet and store it for future projects. Instead of weeding it the other way, take the letters off the sheet. Crack the sheet by bending it, then start lifting off the letters using a pair of tweezers.

Here is the design fully weeded and ready for application. Remove all the excess material; only what is needed should remain transferred.

This includes the centers of letters, which may require reverse weeding. Make sure the centers of letters and any other elements you want on your mouse pad are still on the Infusible Ink sheet. Align the edges with those of the mouse pad and use tape to secure it in place.

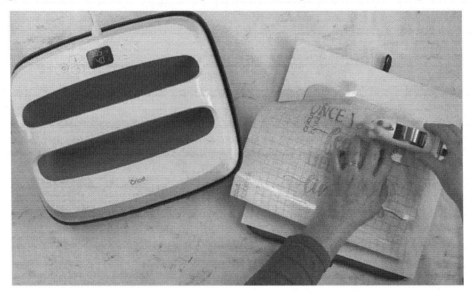

Here is my easy press mat and a piece of cardstock to protect the easy press. The tape doesn't stick well on the mouse pad so stick it on the cardstock. Once you have it all taped down, put down the butcher's paper and place the Easy press on it. Press the button and down with medium pressure for 40 seconds.

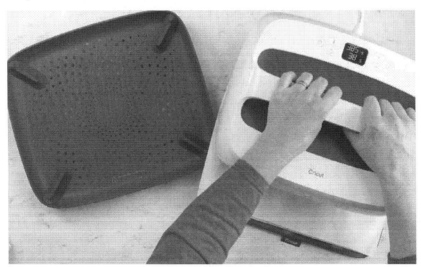

Once your press is complete, lift straight up and allow everything to cool completely. When it is cool, lift the transfer sheet, and pull off the tape to see your design on the mouse pad.

Chapter 10

Jewelry Making

Customized Bracelet Cuffs

Materials Needed

- o Cricut machine
- o Cricut easy press mini
- o Heat transfer vinyl
- o Cricut light grip mat
- o Leather bracelets
- o Wedding tool
- o Scissors
- o Parchment paper

Instructions

Open a new canvas on design space. Click on the text tool and type 'Be The Light'. Change the font by selecting a font from the font icon. Type the second phrase 'Be still and know'. Select a script font for this. Adjust the spacing between the letters by pressing down the arrow on the letter spacing icon on the top menu. If the letters are still not connected for the script font, click 'ungroup' and manually move the letters until they connect.

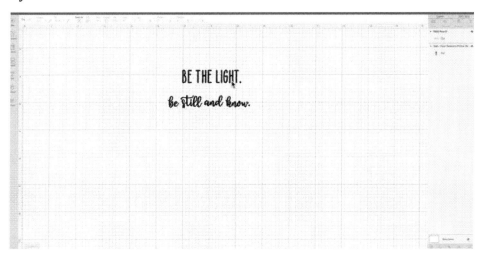

Resize the phrases appropriately to fit the bracelets. Make the first phase to be 0.5 inches in height and 2.75 inches in length. The second phrase should be 0.5 inches in height and 3 inches in length.

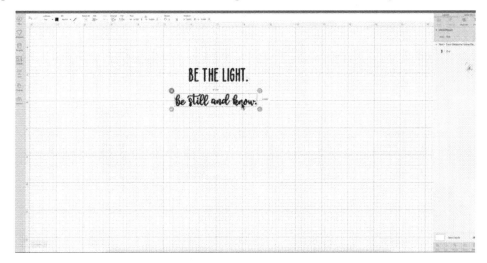

Highlight all the text and click on 'attach'. Click 'Make It'. Mirror the text and move the design to where you want it on the mat in the mat preview screen and click 'continue'.

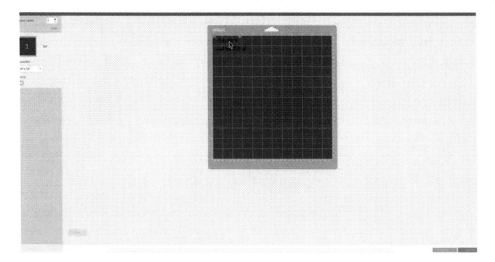

Set your material to an everyday iron-on.

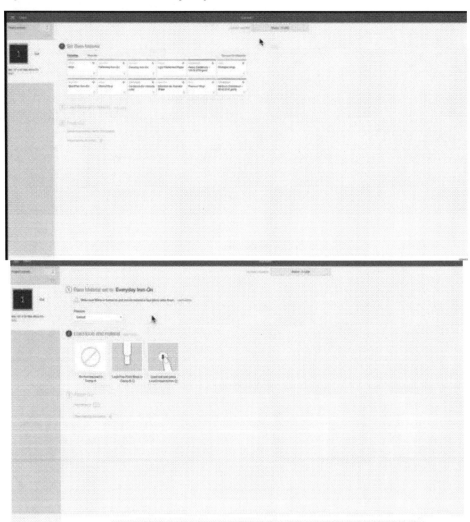

Place the heat transfer vinyl on the mat with the shiny side down in the upper left-hand corner.

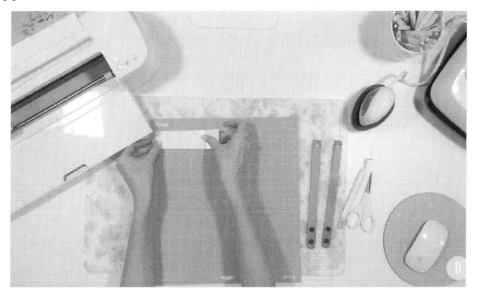

Place it in the Cricut for cutting.

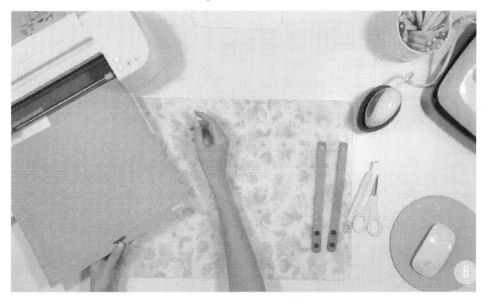

Use the Cricut heat guide to determine the heat settings on your Cricut Easy Press mini. Select the easy press mini in the tool setting and faux leather as the base material. Click 'apply.'

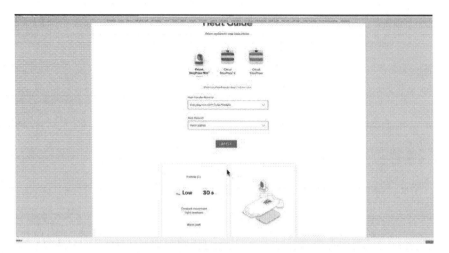

Take off the design from the mat and weed carefully. Remove all the middle letter pieces.

Trim the excess around the design using a scissor and snip between the letters on both edges.

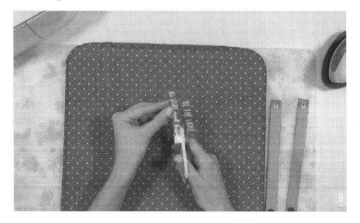

The easy press mini is preheated, set the machine to low and preheat the waistband for 5 seconds.

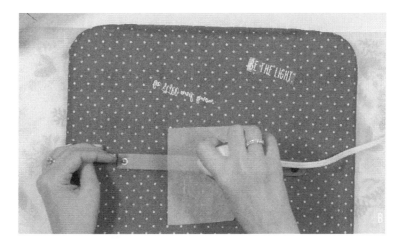

Center the design on the bracelet, place parchment paper over the design, and press for 30 seconds with constant movement and pressure.

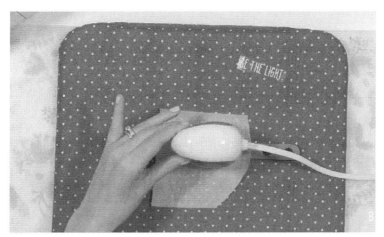

Set it aside to cool and then peel back the tape.

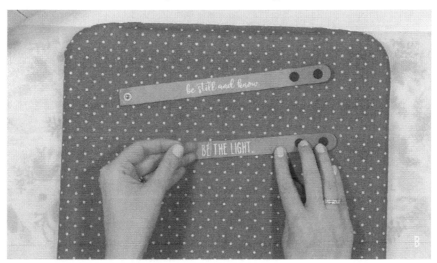

Engraved Pendant Necklaces

Materials Needed

- Cricut machine
- Cricut strong grip mat
- Blanks
- Crystal setting kit
- A pair of tweezers
- Stamp enamel marker
- ImpressArt Hammer
- Stamping block
- stamp enamel maker (black)
- A chain necklace
- Jump rings
- Jewelry pliers
- Birthmark stones gems (three different sizes)
- Round metal Blanks (1 inch & 0.75 inch)
- Transfer tape
- Craft glue

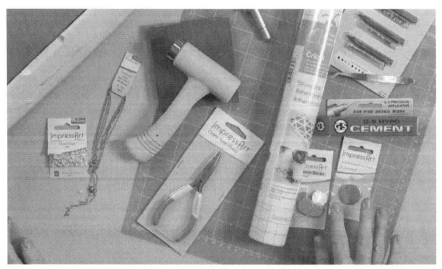

Instructions

Open a new canvas on the design space, click on shapes, select a circle, and duplicate it. These will serve as the metal blanks for the pendant. Resize them to the size of the blanks (1 inch & 0.75 inches).

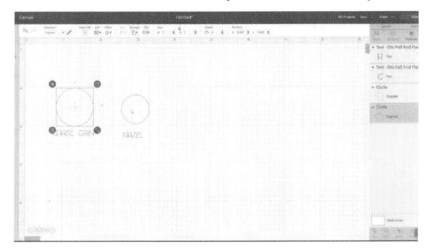

Click on the text icon and type 'Chase Cain & Hazel.' Select a writing font. To find writing fonts go to cricut fonts, click filter, and select writing. Choose the font you like. In this project, I used DTC fall and flair. Make the fonts fairly small like 9.5 because these two are going to be stacked on top of each other. Ensure that the writing does not extend over the other and it does not overlap.

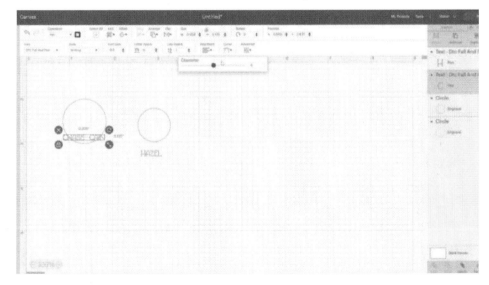

Adjust the fonts to fit inside the circles. Drag the font onto the larger circle and choose the curve option. Opt for a negative curve to have it wrap around the circle. Experiment with the curvature and diameter until you achieve the desired appearance. Repeat the process with the smaller circle. I ended up with different curvatures for both circles: 0.721 for the larger one and 0.421 for the smaller one. There's no need to click 'attach;' leave it as engraving lines. Select the fonts and choose engrave.

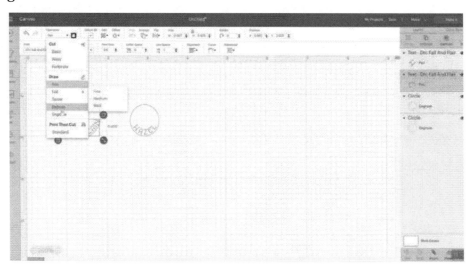

Click 'Make It'. Let's take a look and see what these mean on the mat.

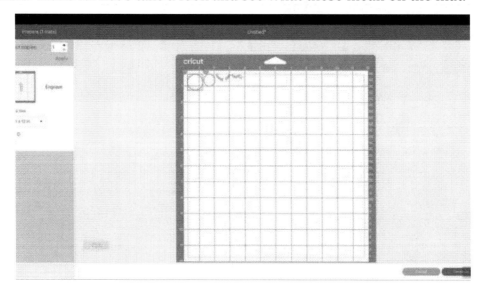

Here are the two circles and the two names. Take the circles and move them to where you are going to put the metal blanks on the mat. Place the first circle at the top of the 1-inch mark and the other circle at the side of the 1-inch mark. Also, move the names into the respective circles. Click on the circles and do 'Hide'.

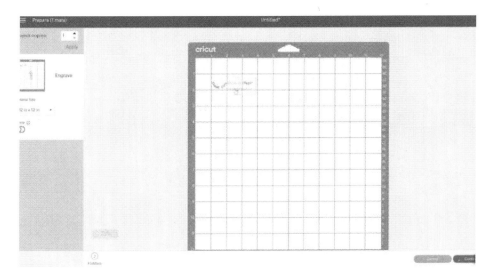

Put the blanks exactly where you had them on this mat, on the actual mat so that when engraving they will be in their correct location. Place a strong grip transfer tape on the strong grip mat and cut a little piece off. You don't need much, it is to ensure that they are stuck down on the mat well. Use a cloth brayer to smooth it down and peel off the backing of the transfer tape.

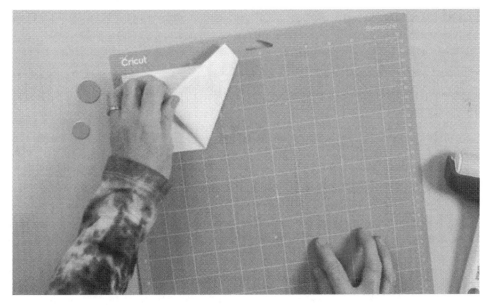

Place the blanks at the designated location on the mat as it was in the design space. Ensure that the holes on the blanks are at the top.

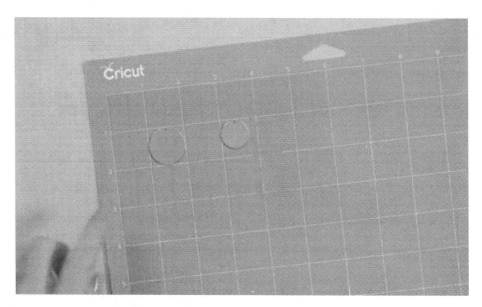

Once these are on the strong grip transfer tape, press down using the brayer again. Go back to the design space and click 'continue'. Once the Cricut is connected, click browse all materials. Select stainless steel and click 'done'.

Set your tools- put the engraving tool in the machine and place your mat to be engraved.

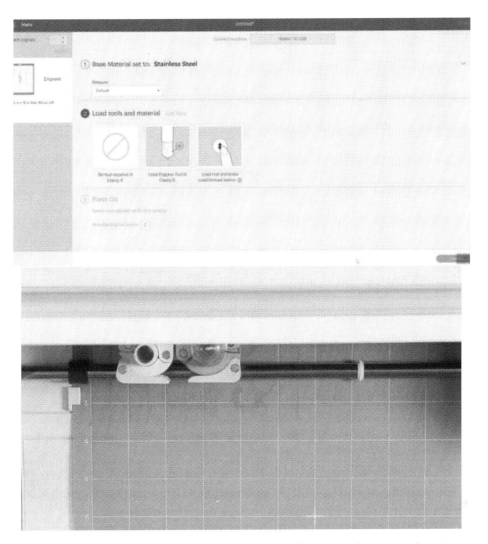

Take out the mat after engraving. Peel up the transfer tape, lay it over the blank and press it down. This picks up any small bits of debris that may have happened during the engraving process. Peel that back and remove it entirely from the mat, popping off your engraved pieces.

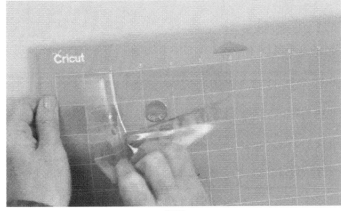

To make the engraving stand out a little more, use the stamp enamel marker to rub it into the engraving.

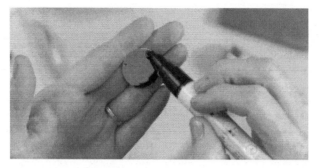

Allow it to sit for a few minutes and then wipe it back off. You will be left with a darker engraving on your piece.

To add intention to the piece, use the middle kit which is 2.5mm stone. Decide where you want to place the stones, I will put two stones at the bottom and one stone at the top. Locate the punch where the stones will be, place the blanks on the stamping block, and strike it with the hammer.

You're simply creating small indentations where the stones will be placed to facilitate the setting process. Repeat this process with the punch and hammer for each stone. After making all the indentations, add a drop of glue to each one and then carefully place each stone in its designated location using a pair of tweezers. Allow it to dry.

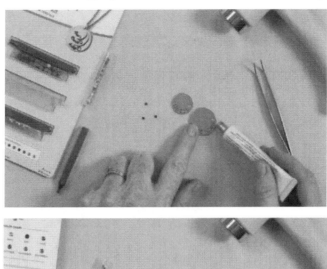

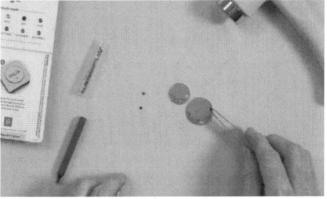

Open the jump ring, add the top piece first and then the bottom piece. Add the entire piece to a chain and close the jump ring.

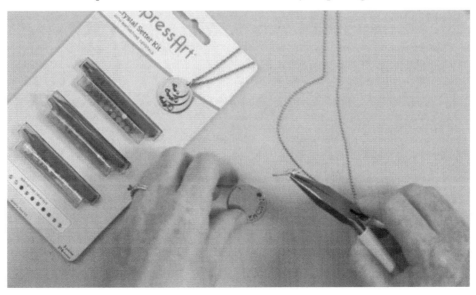

225

Personalized Earring Display Cards

Materials Needed

- o Cricut machine
- o Cricut light grip mat
- o Cardstock

Instructions

Open a new canvas in the design space and click on 'images.'

Go to the search bar and type 'Label'. A bunch of labels will be displayed.

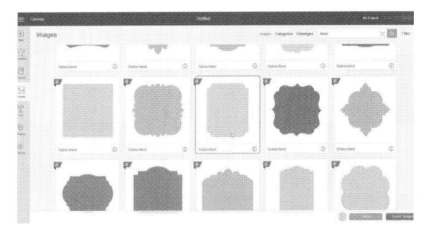

Choose from these or you can click on 'shapes' and select a square. For this project, I chose this one, and click 'add to canvas.'

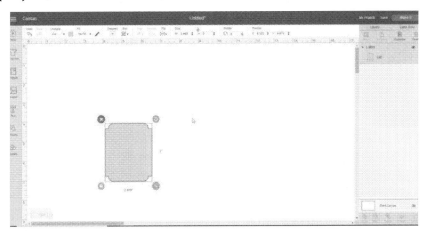

Click on the shape icon and select a circle. Unlock the circle and turn it into an oval.

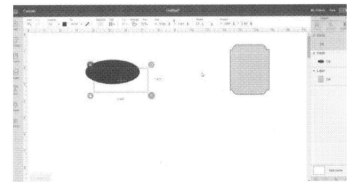

Click on duplicate to make an exact copy, change the color of the duplicate to white and place it on top of the black oval to cover it, leaving a little black part on both sides of the oval. Click out, select the image, and go to slice.

227

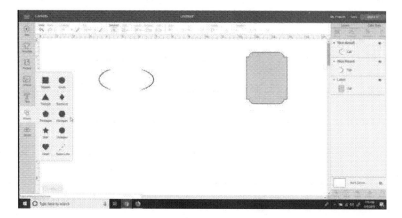

Go back to shapes and click on a circle. Resize it to be very tiny. This will be the hole to put the earring through. Click on the image and tap duplicate.

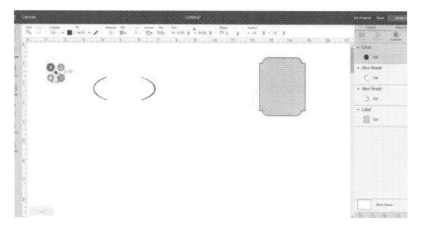

Use the grid lines to determine where the center is and place them on the card.

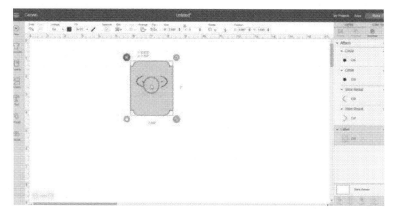

At the top of the card, add text, maybe a business name or logo. Go to text and type' I create crafts.' Resize the text to fit into the top of the card.

Select the image and resize it and click 'attach.' Select the image go up to align and then center it. Click 'Make It' and then tap Continue.

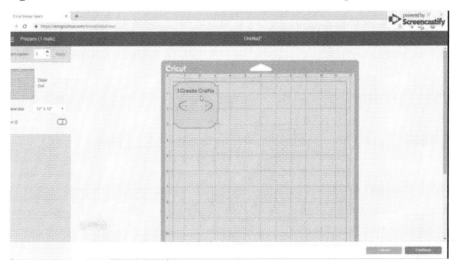

Set the material - cardstock and tools- deep point blade. Place the cardstock on the mat and put it in the cutting machine to cut.

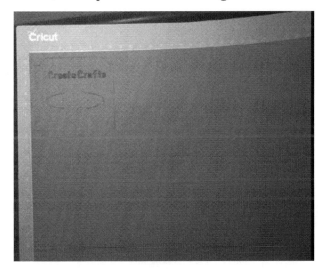

After cutting, take it off the mat by carefully peeling it off.

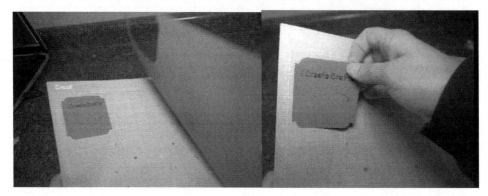

Chapter 11

Pet Accessories

Customized Pet Bowls

Materials Needed

- o Oracal 651 permanent adhesive vinyl
- o Sublimation blank dog bowls
- o Cricut machine
- o Cricut cutting mat
- o Transfer tape
- o Wedding tool
- o Scraper
- o Scissors
- o Denatured alcohol
- o Paper trimmer

Instructions

Open in a new canvas in Cricut design space. Click 'text' and type 'Dinner'. Go to the font and select a font called Dtc Peach Cake. It is part of Cricut Access if you are a member. Resize the height of the text to 2 inches and 6.5 inches in width.

The bowls measure about 7-8 inches in width and I don't want the word to wrap too far around the bowl. Change the color to pink.

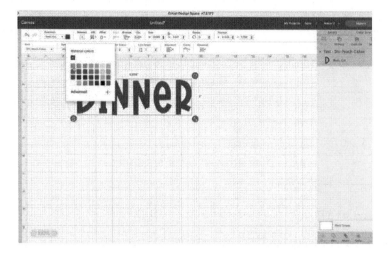

Click on 'text' again and type 'cocktail'. Change to the same font as the 'Dinner'. Resize the word to be 2 inches tall making it 9.5 inches wide. This is too wide for the bowl and wraps too far around it. Go to the letter spacing icon and pull the letters a little bit closer until you get to 7.8 inches. Change the color to pink.

Put a weeding box around the vinyl when cutting it. To do this, go to shapes, select a square, right-click on it and send it to the back.

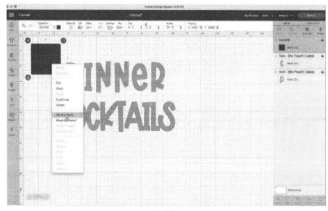

232

You don't need the box to be big, select the box, click the unlock button and move the box in, it doesn't need to be exact.

Highlight the entire design and click 'attach'. This is going to keep everything together and make them the same color.

Click 'Make It'. Select cutting on the mat and click 'continue'.

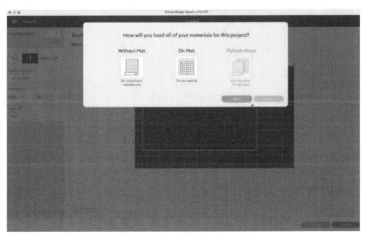

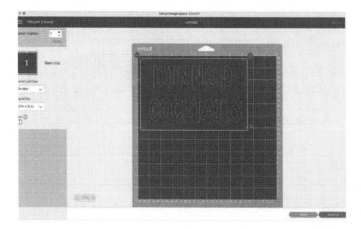

Cut the vinyl to approximately 7 inches by 10 inches. Place it on the mat with the shiny side up.

Go back to Cricut design space and set your base material to premium vinyl permanent glossy.

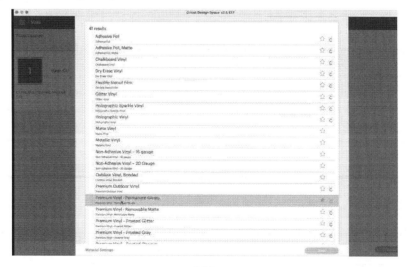

Ensure the fine point blade is in the machine. Place the mat in the cutting machine.

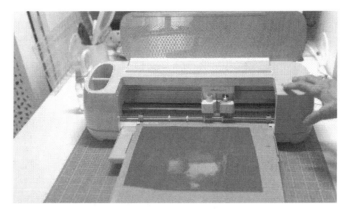

Take some denatured alcohol to clean the blank bowls with a little free cloth. This helps the adhesive stick well. After cutting, weed the design on the mat, and use the scraper to make sure it adhered well. Then grab the corner of that box I made and peel this back.

Weed out the center letters and the design off the mat. Trim around the design and separate it into two pieces.

Place your design back on the mat to keep it flat. Cut a piece of transfer tape enough to cover the design and place it on top of your design. Use a scraper to smooth it down, flip it, and press down too.

To remove the tape, peel it off slowly from the back while keeping the transfer tape flat. This way, if something starts to come off, you can easily push it back down.

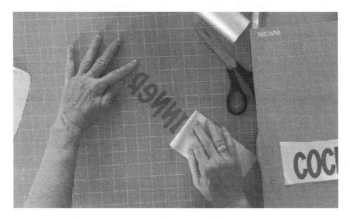

Take a pair of scissors and snip at the top and bottom of the design to allow it to bend.

Position the design on the bowl, ensure it is straight, and from the center press down to the edges. Use the scraper to press it down and then peel it back.

Repeat the same step for the cocktail design.

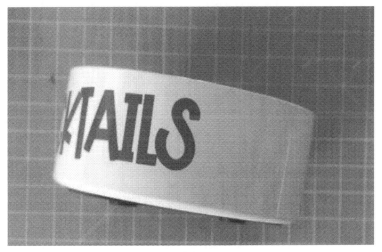

Allow the design to dry for at least 48 hours. Do not wash the bowls in a dishwasher. Hand wash so the design will last longer.

DIY Pet Clothing

Materials Needed

- o Cricut rainbow reflective iron-on
- o Cricut machine
- o Cricut cutting mat
- o Gray dog shirt
- o Measuring tape
- o Cricut auto press
- o Weeding tool

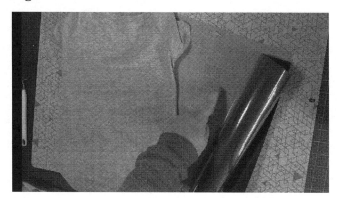

Instructions

Measure the shirt to determine the size of my design.

Open a new canvas in the Cricut design space and click on images. Type in the search bone and paw prints. Select the images you like and click 'add to canvas'. Click on the text icon and type 'will sit for treats'. Choose and font at the top menu. Arrange the text and the images how you want it to look.

Use the line spacing icon to reduce the spacing between the letters and the lines and resize your design to fit on the shirt accordingly.

Tap on 'attach'.

Tap on 'Make It'. Mirror the image on the mat preview screen,

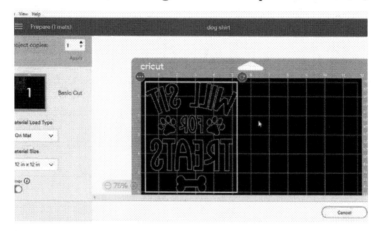

select 'with mat' and click 'continue'. Set your base material by clicking 'browse all materials'. Select reflective iron-on.

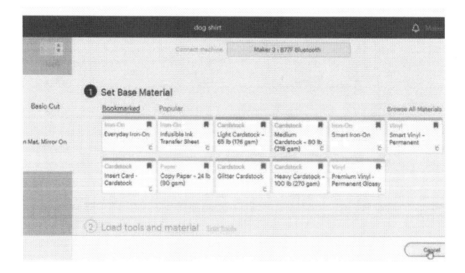

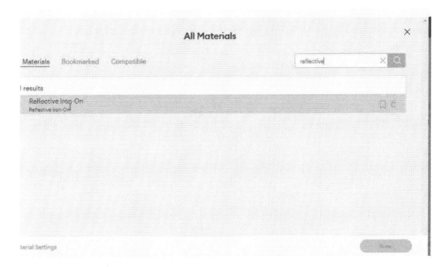

Peel off the protective sheet of the cutting mat. There is a shiny side and a dull side of this iron-on, put the shiny side down on the cutting mat and place it in the Cricut machine.

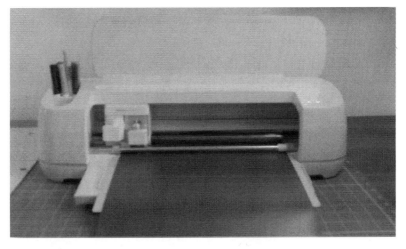

After cutting, flip your mat over and pull the mat away from the material. Trim and weed your design.

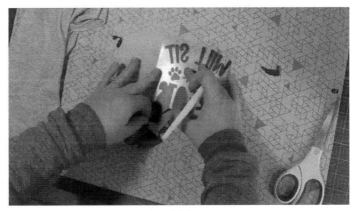

Set the auto press to 330° for 30 seconds.

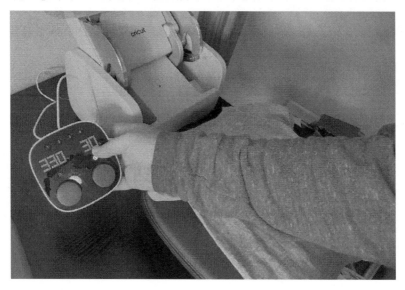

Preheat the shirt for 5 seconds and then place the design on the shirt and lower the auto press.

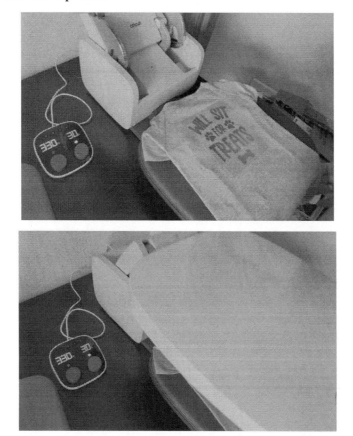

Once it is done, allow it to cool and then peel back the protective sheet.

Personalized Pet Pillow Covers

Materials Needed

- o Cricut machine
- o Cricut cutting mat
- o Plain white pillow cover
- o Heat transfer vinyl
- o Cricut auto press
- o Weeding tool

Instructions.

Go to cutecutters.com, this is the website you will use to upload your pet photo and convert it into an SVG file. Upload your pet photo, adjust the settings on the side until the picture looks the way you want it.

When it is done, remove the background and save the image on your desktop.

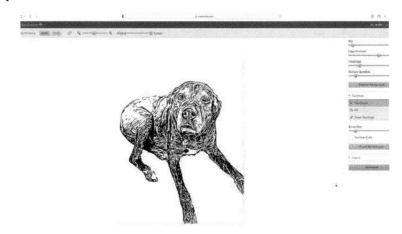

Open design space and upload the image by dragging and dropping it. Click on your picture that you want to insert into the canvas onto design space.

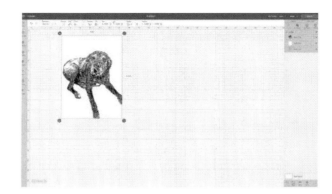

The imported image from Cute Cutter has two background layers, one is pink and the other is white. Turn both background layers off because it is not needed in this project. Click on text and type 'Lola'.

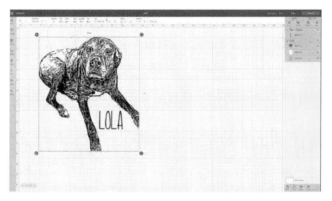

Change the font and click 'weld'. Save your design and click 'Make It'. Mirror your design on the preview screen and click 'continue'.

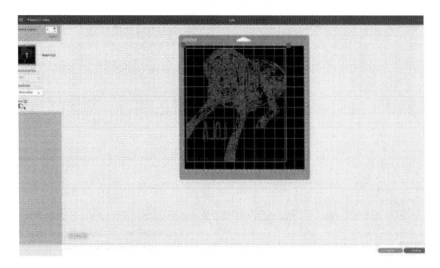

Set your base material to 'everyday iron- on'.

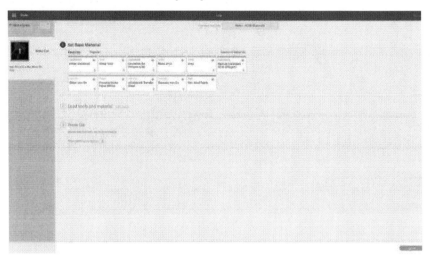

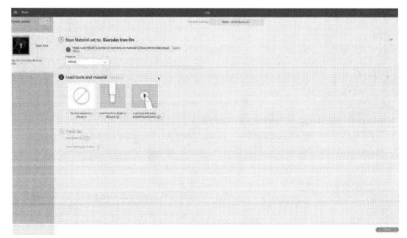

Place the heat transfer vinyl on the mat and put it in the cutting machine.

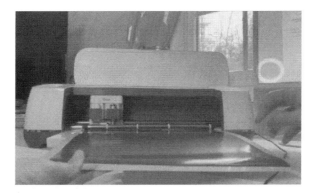

After cutting, weed out the negative vinyl from your design.

Prepare the pillow cover and preheat for 5 seconds at 305°. Place the design on the pillow cover and press for 15 seconds at 305°.

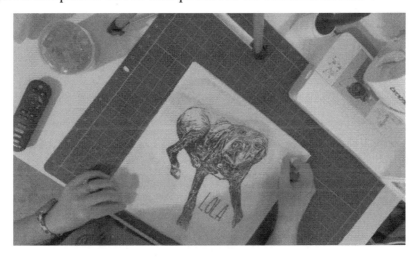

Allow it to cool and peel off the protective sheet.

Pet Collar Embellishments

Materials Needed

- o Cricut Machine
- o Cricut standard grip mat
- o Blank Martingale collar
- o Infusible ink transfer sheet
- o Wedding tool
- o Scissors

Instructions

Open a new canvas in design space. Click on shapes and select a heart. Click on the text icon and type 'My Motley'. Arrange the shape and text to read ' ♥ my Motley Mutt'. Resize your design to fit the width of the webbing of the collar. The collar is 0.75 inches webbing and the height is 0.55.

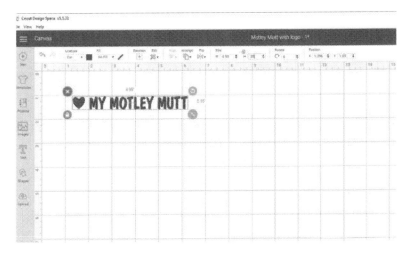

Select everything and click 'attach' and then click 'Make It'. Turn the mirror on and click 'continue'.

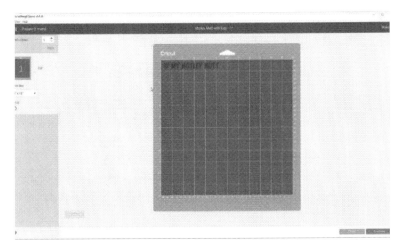

Set your base material to an infusible ink sheet and set your tools- fine point blade and select 'more pressure.'

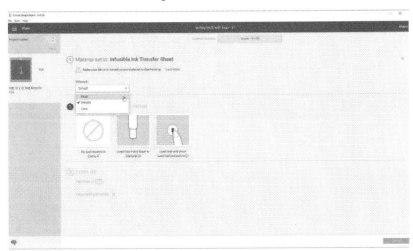

Position the infusible ink transfer sheet on a standard grip mat with the right side facing up. Then, insert it into the cutting machine to begin the cutting process.

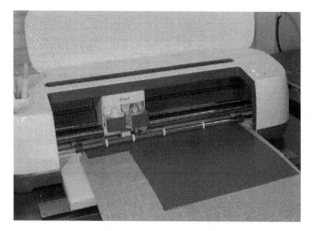

After cutting, remove the mat from the machine. Flip the mat over and peel away the mat.

Trim the design into two parts for easy weeding and application. Gently weed your design.

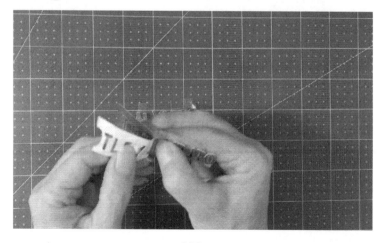

Set the Cricut Easy press to 380° for 40 seconds. Place a butcher paper on the collar and Preheat for 15 seconds. Place the design on the collar, cover it with butcher paper and press for 40 seconds.

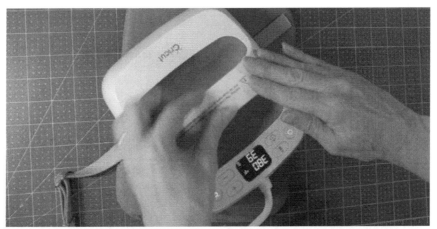

Gardening and Planters

Custom Planters

Material Needed

- o Plain plant pots

- o Isopropyl Alcohol

- o Measuring tape

- o Paper towels

- ○ Cricut machine
- ○ Permanent Vinyl
- ○ Wedding tool
- ○ Scissors
- ○ Transfer tape
- ○ Scraper

Instructions

Use a clean towel and apply Isopropyl Alcohol on the pot's exterior to remove dust and fingerprints.

In Cricut Design Space, open a new canvas and click on the text icon. Type "kind of a big" and "Here for a good". Choose a thick and bold font, then adjust the letter spacing as needed.

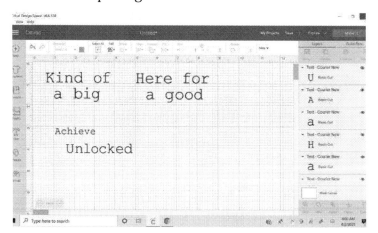

Click on 'text' again and type 'Dill, Thyme & mint.' Use a script font and adjust the spacing between the letters until they are close to each other.

Use a measuring tape to measure the pot's surface area and adjust the text size accordingly. Place the vinyl on the cutting mat, adjust the Cricut dial to "vinyl" and initiate the cutting process.

After cutting, take off the mat and carefully peel the vinyl by placing the mat face down and gently separating it from the vinyl to avoid any damage. Weed the design by eliminating the unnecessary cut sections of vinyl. Also, remove all the centers of the letters.

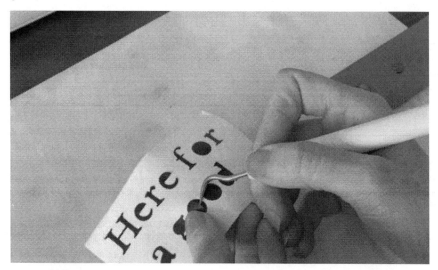

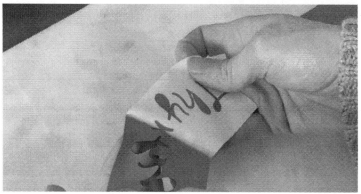

Trim a piece of transfer tape to match your design size. Remove the backing and adhere it to the vinyl. Burnish the tape's top, using a scraper ensuring the elimination of any air bubbles or ruffles.

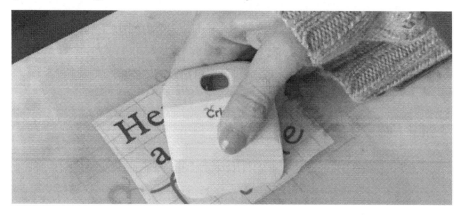

Remove the vinyl backing.

Attach the design to the pot plant, smoothen it and then carefully peel off the transfer tape. Ensure the design lays flat without any creases. Peel away the transfer tape and the design will be visible on the pot plant. Repeat the above step with the remaining designs.

Garden Stepping Stones

Materials Needed

- Concrete stepping stone paver (12x12 inches)

- Outdoor spray paint in clear coat (green, blue, red, black, and pink)

- Cricut stencil film or other Cricut vinyl

- Cricut transfer tape

- Cricut scraper

Instructions

Open a new canvas on the design space and click on images. Go to the Cricut access search bar and Type 'flowers.' Select this flower design (#M4ADFB110) and click 'add to Canvas'.

Change the colors of the layers. Add registration marks to layer the vinyl by clicking on the shape icon to insert a triangle beneath your design Use a couple of triangles one for each color of vinyl, such as green, pink, blue, red and dotted black in this project. Highlight all five triangles and click align center the three triangles so that they stack directly on top of each other. Make a copy of this stack and place it two inches to the right of the first copy. Align them to be on the same plane, click center vertically and nudge them up and next to your pattern. Highlight each element of the same color and then unite them together so that when you cut it, everything is arranged the way it should be.

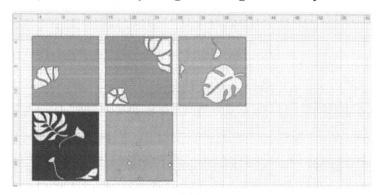

Click 'Make It'. Preview the mat screen and click 'continue.' Set your materials and tools. Place the Cricut stencil film or other Cricut vinyl on the mat and put it in the machine to cut. After cutting, remove the vinyl from the mat and weed your designs.

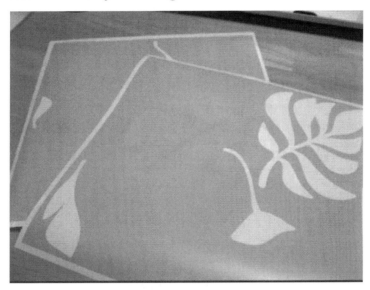

Prepare your concrete stepping stone or paver for stenciling by administering multiple base coats of clear or colored paint. This process serves to seal the concrete and establish a more even surface for applying your stencil. Ensure adequate drying time.

Using transfer tape, place the first stencil onto the prepared stone. Burnish the vinyl well with a scraping tool so that there are no gaps or bubbles when it sticks to the stone.

Using a stencil, apply multiple thin layers of spray paint on a covered surface while working outside, then let it dry. Take off the first stencil that is on the stone. Next, lightly spray on many coats of clear spray and let them dry completely.

Repeat with all of the stencils you made for each paint layer.

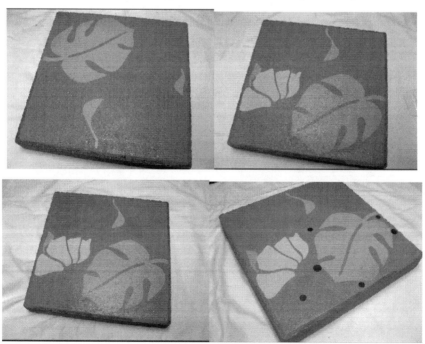

Give the stone ample time to dry for several days before introducing it to the elements in the garden.

DIY Seed Starter Pots

Materials Needed

- o Cricut Explore Air 2
- o Cricut Permanent Vinyl
- o Cricut Transfer Tape
- o Cricut Tools and Blue Mat
- o Garden Pots

Instructions

Open a new canvas in the Cricut design space and click on the text tool. Type 'succ it, Aloe you vera much, I wet my plants. Use a different font for each phrase and adjust both the line and letter spacings between each phrase by using the line spacing icon on the top menu or highlighting each phrase and clicking 'ungroup' to move the letters and line spacings closer. Measure the garden pot surface area to know how big or small to adjust the design. Resize the texts accordingly to fit in front of the pots. Click 'Make It' and then 'Continue'. Set your base material to permanent vinyl and your tools. Place the vinyl on the cutting mat and put it in the Cricut to cut. After cutting, remove the mat and weed your design.

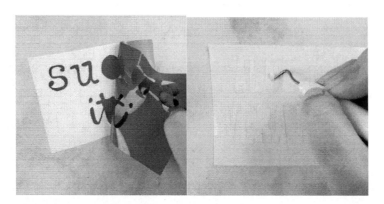

Cover the words with a piece of transfer tape and firmly scrape it down for effective adhesion.

Ensure the pot is thoroughly cleaned; apply rubbing alcohol to eliminate any grease or grime that might hinder the proper adhesion of the vinyl.

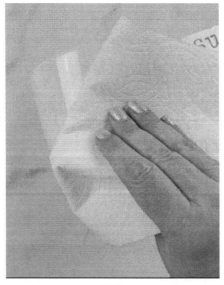

Remove the backing, position it on the pot as desired, firmly scrape it down, and then peel off the transfer tape for a clean application.

Allow it to dry for 72 hours before exposing it to moisture to ensure a premium bond with the adhesive.

Add a plant to the pot and enjoy your newly adorned garden pots.

Chapter 12

Art and Creativity

Customized Art Prints

Materials Needed

- o Cricut machine
- o Cricut strong grip mat
- o Cricut foil transfer tool
- o Cricut foil transfer sheets
- o Special formulated Tape
- o Art frame hanger
- o Craft glue

Instructions

Open a new project in the Cricut design space and click on images. Type 'skull' in the search bar and select any one of your choice. For this project, I chose a detailed skull image with the number M17F8D593. Click 'add to canvas'.

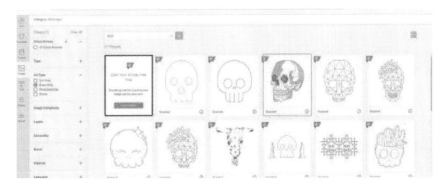

Choose 'Draw Only' from the Art Type menu in the left sidebar, showing exclusively single-line drawings. For optimal foil artwork translation, single-line drawings are recommended, as standard cut files might convert with double lines, outlining each stroke.

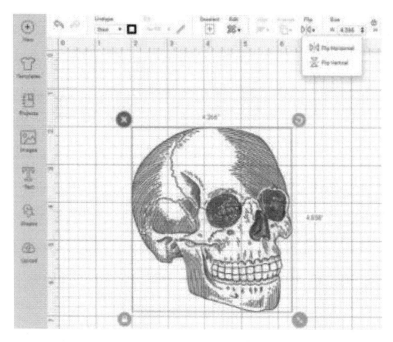

Position the skull to face right, by clicking on the top toolbar to horizontally flip the selected image. Afterward, adjust the image size accordingly to fit your artwork.

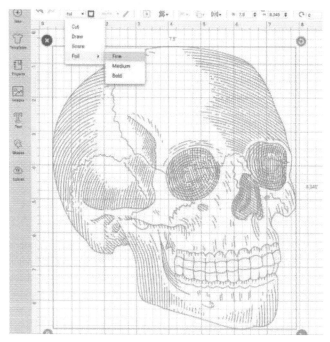

Adjust the line type to 'Foil' and pick your preferred line width from the drop-down menu. The foil lines will automatically appear in gold; modify the foil color if needed. Once the image is appropriately sized and colored, click 'Make It'.

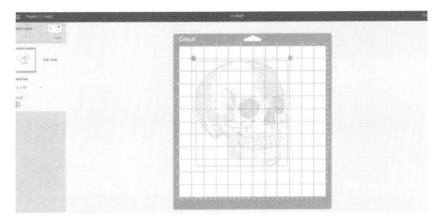

Ensure your design is positioned away from the edges of the mat. For optimal results with Foil Transfer Sheets, maintain a minimum 1/4" margin between the foil edges and your design. Allow space for taping the foil to your material, as any tape covering your design may hinder proper foil transfer in those areas.

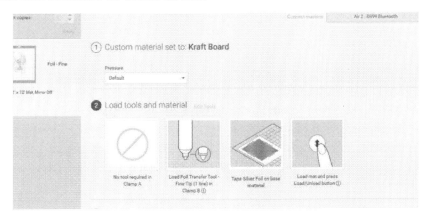

Pick your base material from the list, cut the Foil Transfer Sheet to size (slightly larger than your design but smaller than the base material) and use the provided tape strips to secure the foil (shiny colored side up) onto the base. Ensure the foil is smooth and firmly secured on all four sides.

Note: Avoid placing the Foil Transfer Sheet directly on your cutting mat to prevent the foil from sticking, which could result in foil particles embedding in the adhesive and transferring to future projects on the same mat.

For a 12x12 material base, use a full large foil sheet without trimming, as it will cover the mat adhesive entirely. Load the mat into the machine and tap the flashing Cricut button to initiate the foiling process.

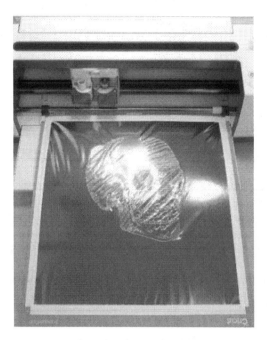

Once the foiling process is finished, carefully remove the tape and peel back the Cricut Foil Transfer Sheet to reveal your remarkable new foil artwork.

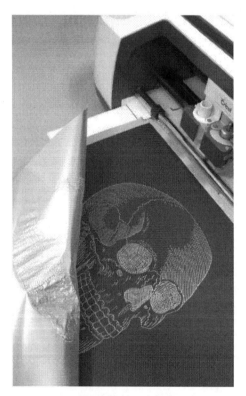

Trim the 12x12 sheet to the desired size using a pair of scissors and add a slim wood backing piece with a gunmetal glitter finish.

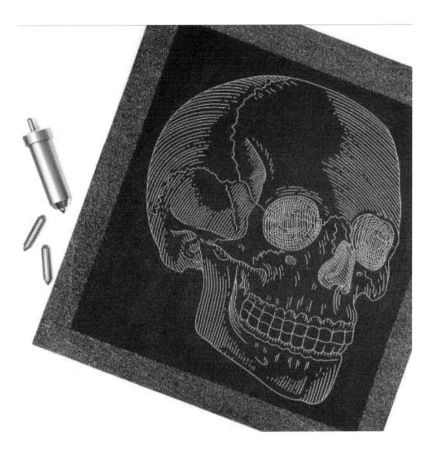

DIY Coloring Books

Materials Needed

- o Cricut machine
- o Cricut light grip mat
- o Copy papers or cardstock
- o Strings
- o Scissors

Instructions

Open a new canvas in the design space and click on images. Select all the images you need for the coloring book and click 'add to canvas.'

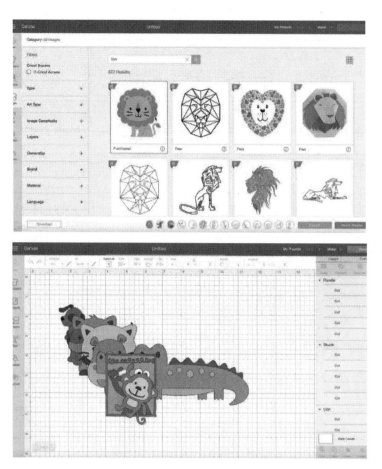

Tap on the shape icon and select a square sliced with two holes equally spaced out.

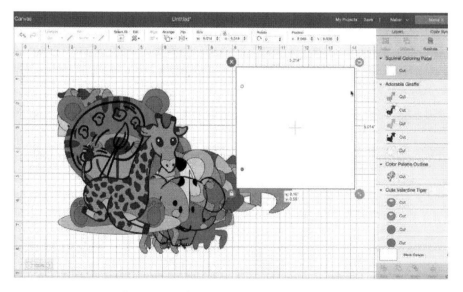

Convert images to draw mode instead of cut. Attach the image to the square. This will tell Cricut to draw and cut the square.

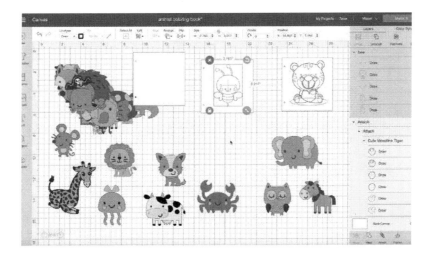

Do this for all your images.

Make a cover page for the book.

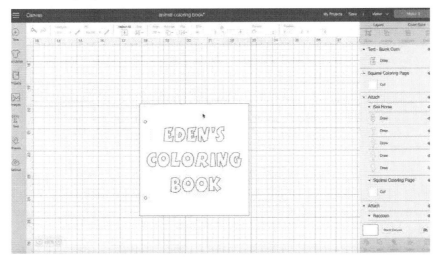

'Click Make it'. Set your base material to copy paper and tools. Place the copy paper on the mat and put it into the cutting machine.

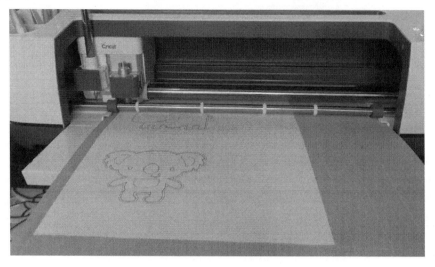

After cutting, trim off the rough edges of the copy papers and arrange them, aligning the two holes by the side.

Take a string and put it through the first hole, leaving a bit hanging out to make room for the sequence. Ensure that the book is nicely aligned. Take the string and make a double knot. Make the knot to be right enough to be able to turn the pages. Pass the string into the second hole through the back, ensure it is lined up, and then put it underneath the first string and pull through. Make a knot at the end.

Take the sequence and thread it into the string. When you are done, knot the tip of the string and cut the excess string.

Crafty Scrapbooks

Material Needed

- o Cricut machine
- o Cricut standard grip mat
- o Card stocks (Yellow, white, orange, blue)
- o Scissors
- o Wedding tool
- o Craft glue

Instructions

Open a new canvas on the design space.

Click on the shape icons and select a square. Resize the square to 8.5 inches by 11 inches. Click on the unlock button and change the size of the square by typing in the figures. Tap on the lock button again so you don't accidentally change the size of the page. Change the color of the page to white.

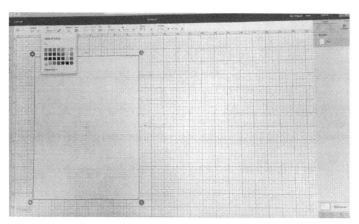

Click on 'text' and type number 3, choose a font and resize it to cover half of the page.

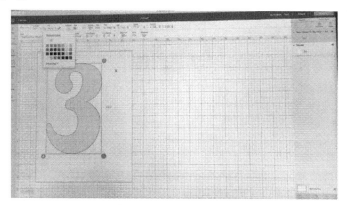

Tap on images and type 'ducks' in the search bar. Select the purple duck.

Click on it and it puts it onto the bottom bar. Click 'Insert Image' and it will be added to the canvas you are working on.

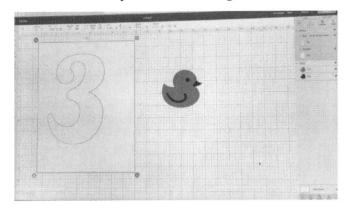

Change the color of the duck to yellow and shrink down the size. Highlight the duck and tap duplicate twice on the top menu to give you a total of three ducks. Move the ducks around where you want to place them and click on the flip button to flip the duck to face the other way. Click 'make it'.

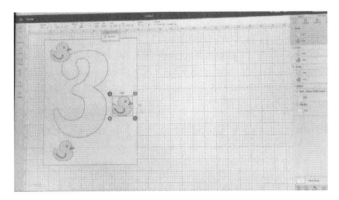

Place the cardstock on the mat and put it in the cutting machine.

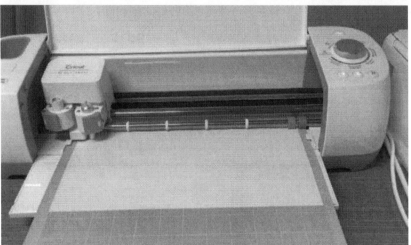

After cutting, weed your designs.

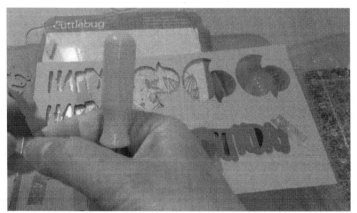

The Cricut machine will cut out the scrapbook page (white and yellow)), the giant number 3, Happy Birthday (orange) and the three little ducks (yellow and orange).

274

Go back to design space, click on the shape icon and select a square. Resize it to 8.5 inches by 11 inches. This will be the second page of the scrapbook. Tap on images and type 'balloons' in the search bar. Select a balloon bouquet and insert it into your canvas.

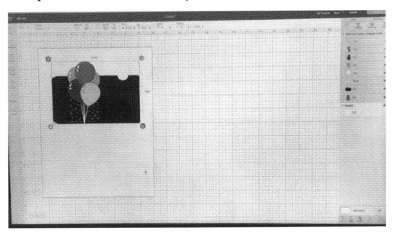

Click on the images you don't want and it will be deleted automatically.

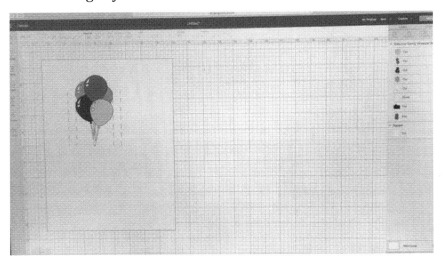

To change the color of the balloons, click on the color you don't want and then go to the color icon and choose a color. Resize the balloon bouquet to fit the page, highlight it and tap 'duplicate'.

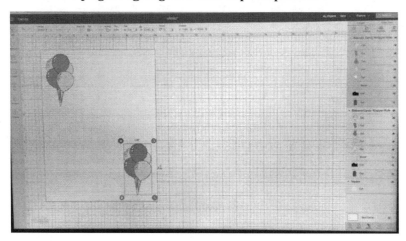

Click 'Make It'.

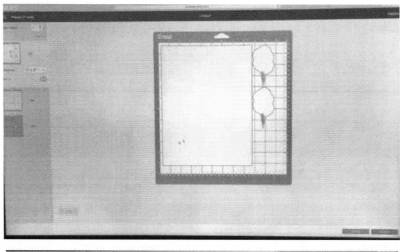

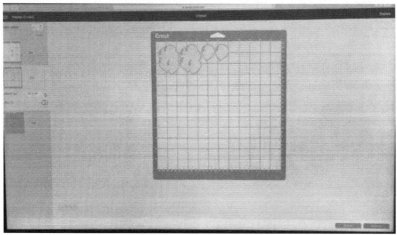

Place the cardstock on the mat and put it in the cutting machine.

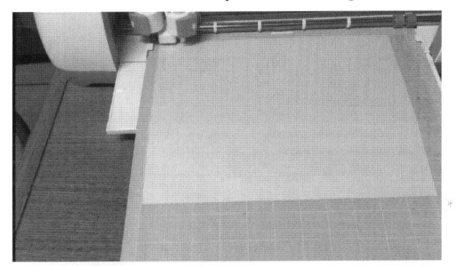

The Cricut will cut the balloons in two colors (blue & yellow).

Glue together the two-layer ducks, the "Happy Birthday," the "Giant 3," and the balloon bouquets to create a sturdy and dimensional appearance. Enhance the balloons with shimmer for texture. Create yellow and blue polka dots using a hole punch and attach them to the page with a small dab of glue.

Here is the finished scrapbook.

Personalized Art Supply Tote Bag

Materials Needed

o   Cricut machine

- Cricut standard grip mat

- Wedding tool

- Scapula

- Scraper

- Scissors

- Large canvas tote bag (43cm×38cm×10cm)

- Cricut EasyPress 2 Heat Press

- Cricut EasyPress Heat Resistant Mat

- Cricut Heat Resistant Tape

- Cricut Iron-On in colors of choice

Instructions

Open a new canvas on design space.

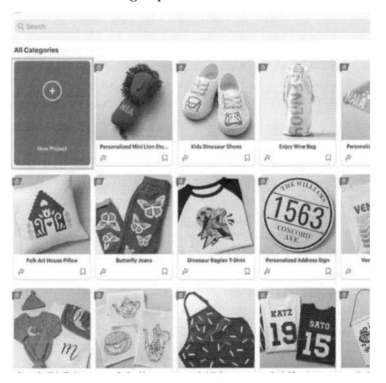

Click on 'images' and type in the numbers below in the search bar. Select each one and click 'insert to canvas'. #M18ECE931, #M7EF6030, #M3DFB9 & #M81B3C1C.

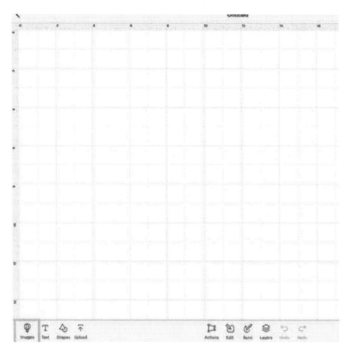

Arrange the designs across the canvas to enable individual editing. Click on each design separately and reposition them. Go to the 'layers' panel for assistance if required.

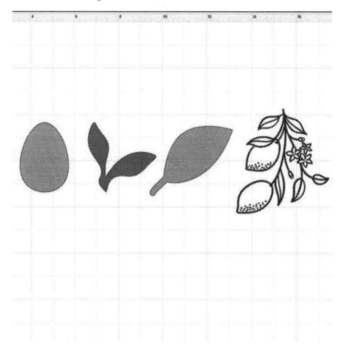

Create a copy of the egg shape by duplicating it. Go to the 'actions' panel and tap 'duplicate' to achieve this.

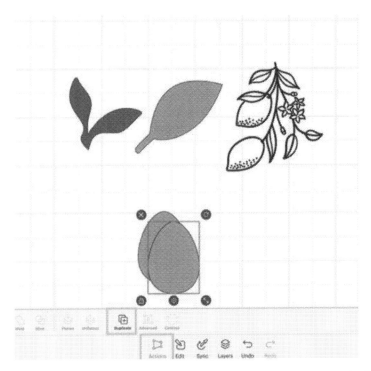

Modify the size of each image as necessary using the 'edit' panel. Highlight one image at a time and adjust either the width or height, following the provided guidelines.

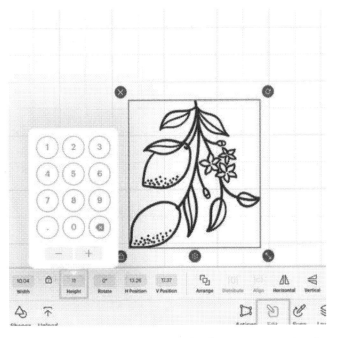

Change the color of the images to match the iron-on vinyl you'll use. Go to the 'actions' panel and click the color circle to access the color drop-down menu for this purpose.

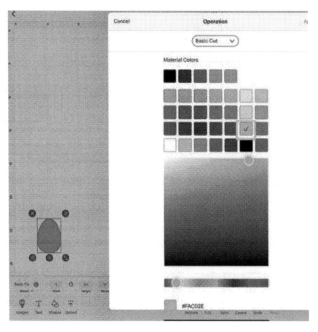

Align and rotate the images appropriately using the 'rotation' icon while selecting each image. If necessary, use the 'edit' panel to send an image behind others in case of incorrect arrangement on the canvas. This step is essential for positioning your cut pieces effectively on your bag.

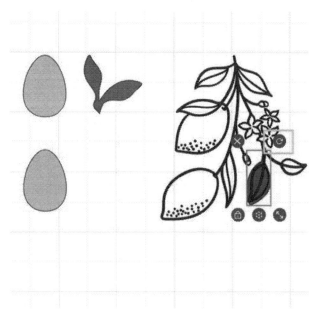

When you are done with the design, click 'make it' and choose 'on the mat'.

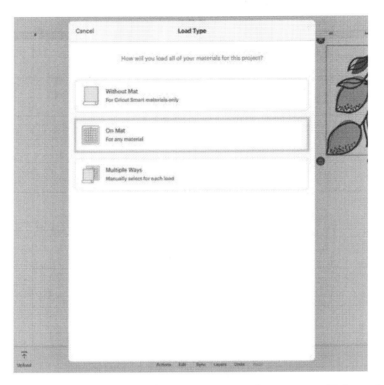

To ensure correct orientation for iron-on applications, click and select 'mirror' on each mat.

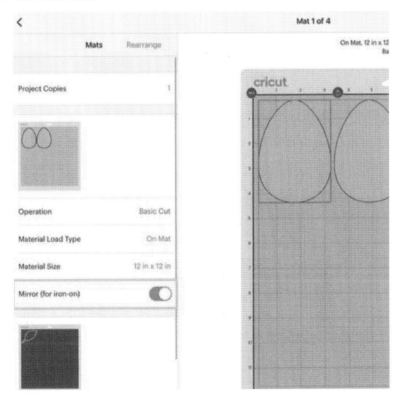

Tap 'continue,' connect to your Cricut machine and choose 'everyday iron-on' as your base material.

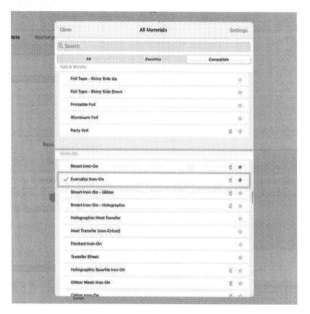

Stick to the on-screen instructions to finalize your cuts. Place the appropriate color iron-on vinyl on the mats, ensuring the shiny side of the vinyl is facing downward.

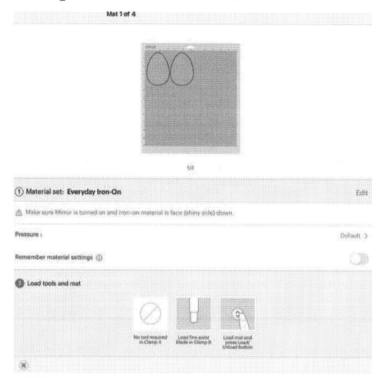

Gather all your cut pieces and trim and weed them as needed.

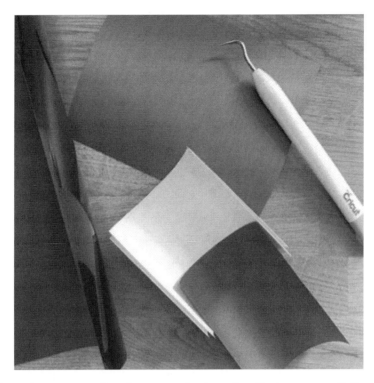

Layer the design with the weeded side facing up, following the arrangement as displayed on the Design Space canvas

Ensure the correct orientation of the designs during the layering process. To ensure that there are no wrinkles or moisture left on the canvas bag, insert the easy press mat inside the bag and preheat the bag before placing the layered design on it.

Carefully peel off the black outline cut layer, leaving the lemons and leaves in their designated positions. Keep them firm with heat-resistant tape if necessary.

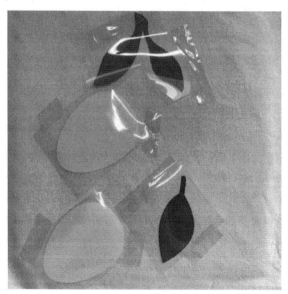

Set the Easy Press temperature to 340°F for 30 seconds Apply the leaves and lemons to the canvas bag using the Easy Press at this temperature.

Place the black outline on top of the bag, aligning it over the lemons and leaves. Refer to the design on the canvas if necessary. Press it into place, ensuring that the lemons and leaves are shielded from direct contact with the heat press. If any part is peeking around the outline's transfer sheet, cover it with a bit of heat tape.

After cooling, remove the transfer sheet and savor the result!

Beauty and Self-Care

Custom Bath Salt Containers

Materials Needed

- o Cricut machine

- o Cricut transfer tape

- o Cricut Mint permanent gloss vinyl

- o Cricut precious metallic textured permanent vinyl

- o An assortment of clean containers

Instructions

Open up a new canvas in the Design Space, click on 'text' and search for the 'Boys Will Be Boys- Block' font.

Enter your label name into the text box.

Highlight the text, go to the 'Edit' menu in the toolbar at the bottom of the screen and adjust both 'Letter Spacing' and 'Line Spacing' to '0'.

Highlight the text, click 'align' and then 'center' to ensure the top line of text is positioned centrally over the top line.

Measure the jar for the label. In Design Space's 'Edit' menu, verify that the text's height and width don't surpass the jar's measurements. Adjust the lettering size by changing the height/width measurement with the padlock icon locked if needed.

Highlight the text and "Ungroup" for each letter group (orange, purple, and blue). Draw a selection box over the label text and tap 'Weld' from the 'Edit' menu.

Go to the 'Edit' menu again, then choose the color swatch next to 'Cut.' Pick a color from the drop-down that closely matches the vinyl color you intend to use for cutting the label.

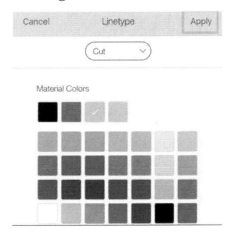

Highlight the label text, go to the 'Actions' menu, and choose 'Duplicate.' Change the color of this duplicated text to match the second vinyl you'll use.

Review everything in the mat preview screen, ensuring accuracy before clicking 'Continue'. Consider adding extra space between labels for easier weeding later. Select each label and shift it slightly on the mat.

Adjust the Air 2 dial to "Custom" (not applicable for Maker or Joy). Choose the vinyl type from the materials setting and follow the prompts displayed on the screen to cut out each label. After cutting all the labels, detach the vinyl from the mat and meticulously separate each label with sharp scissors. Proceed to weed each label using a weeding tool. Use Transfer Tape to attach the base layer of each label onto the jars. Subsequently, apply the top layer, slightly offsetting to the right for a visible portion of the bottom vinyl layer.

Employ a scraper tool for optimal vinyl adhesion to the glass jar. Remove the Transfer Tape gradually and at a 45-degree angle. The jars are ready to be displayed in your bathroom.

Customized Hair Brushes

Materials Needed

- Hairbrush
- Permanent Vinyl
- Transfer Tape
- Cricut Joy (Any Cricut will do!)
- Cricut tools
- Measuring tape

Instructions

Measure the back of the brush to determine how big the name will be. Open a new canvas in the design space, click on 'shapes', and select a circle. Turn the circle into an oval and adjust the size of the oval to be the same dimension as the hairbrush. Click on 'text' and type the name 'Iyleah'.

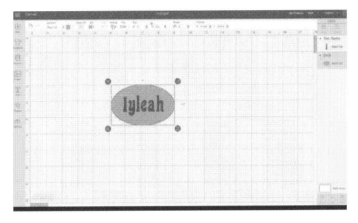

Change the font and resize the text to fit inside the oval. Click 'contour' and then 'hide' to remove the oval. Tap 'attach' and click 'make It'. Select 'without Mat' and set your material - permanent vinyl. Ensure your Cricut is connected and place the vinyl in it to cut.

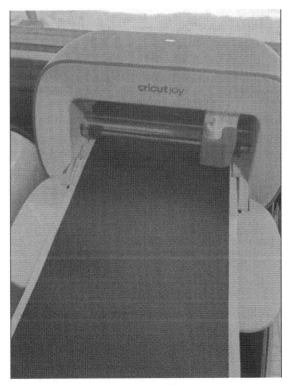

After cutting, weed your design. Use transfer tape to place on top of your design and press it down using a scraper. Peel off the backing.

Place the design at the back of the brush, press it down using the scraper and peel back the transfer tape, leaving your design on the hairbrush.

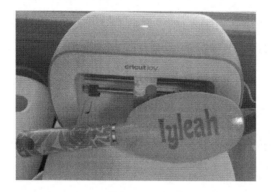

Vinyl Stickers for Makeup Organizers

Materials Needed

- o Mason jars
- o Cricut machine
- o Black permanent vinyl
- o Scraper
- o Weeding tool
- o Transfer paper
- o Rubbing alcohol
- o Rice

Instructions

Open a new canvas in the design space, click on images, and type 'makeup'. Select images like a makeup brush, lips and eyes. Click 'add to canvas.'

Measure your jars to determine how big the stickers will be. Resize the images and click 'Make It'.

Set your material to permanent vinyl and ensure your Cricut is connected. Place the vinyl in the cutting machine to cut. After cutting, weed your design and remove the excess around the design as well as any pieces in the middle as shown below. Clean the jar using rubbing alcohol to remove any dust with a lint-free cloth. Cut a piece of transfer tape and place it on top of the design. Press it down using a scraper and gently peel off the design. Position the design on the jar, press it down using a scraper, and peel it off at 45°, leaving your design on the jar. Repeat these steps with the other two images.

Fill the jars with rice almost to the brim and add all your makeup pieces and brushes.

Personalized Compact Mirrors

Materials Needed

- o Small compact mirror
- o Holographic Vinyl
- o Cutting machine
- o Transfer tape
- o Weeding tool
- o Scissors
- o Ruler

Instructions

Measure the surface of the compact mirror to determine the size of the design. Open a new canvas in the design space, click on 'text' and type 'Boss Babe'. Change the font, and use the line and letter spacing icons to reduce the spacing between each letter and line. Resize to fit the compact mirror.

Click on 'shapes' and select a square. This will serve as a weeding box. Resize the square and place the text into the square. 'Click 'weld' and then 'Make it'. Place the vinyl on the mat and cut the design with your Cricut machine. Weed the vinyl by pulling away the excess vinyl so you are left with your desired text.

Trim a piece of transfer tape to match your design size. Remove the backing and adhere it to the vinyl. Burnish the tape's top, using a scraper ensuring the elimination of any air bubbles or ruffles. Attach the design to the compact mirror, smoothen it and then carefully peel off the transfer tape. Ensure the design lays flat without any creases. Peel away the transfer tape.

Chapter 13

Educational Aids

Spelling Games

Material Needed

- o Cricut machine (Explorer Air 2, Explorer 3, Maker and Maker 3)
- o Cricut standard grip mat
- o Dry-erase board (10 inches × 14 inches)
- o Rubbing alcohol
- o Coffee filter
- o Oracle 651 vinyl (matte finish)
- o Transfer tape
- o Cricut cutter
- o Wedding tool
- o Scraper
- o Spatula

Instructions

For this project, we will create a word search that includes all the names of the family members. Go to 'The Word Search' website, type 'Family' in the title box, and then type all the names of your Mom's family members including her children and grandchildren.

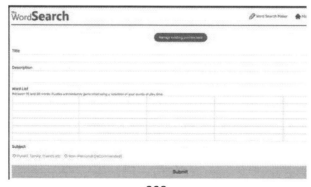

When you are done, tap on 'non-personal' and click 'submit'. A neat preview screen is displayed, click 'download/ print'. Download it as an image and save it to your computer.

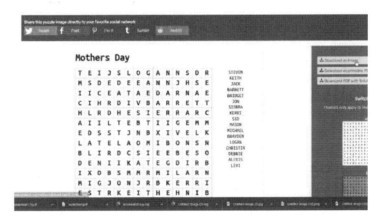

Right-click 'save as' and click 'save next'.

Go to 'upload image', browse and select your file. Click 'open', tap on 'simple' and then click 'continue'.

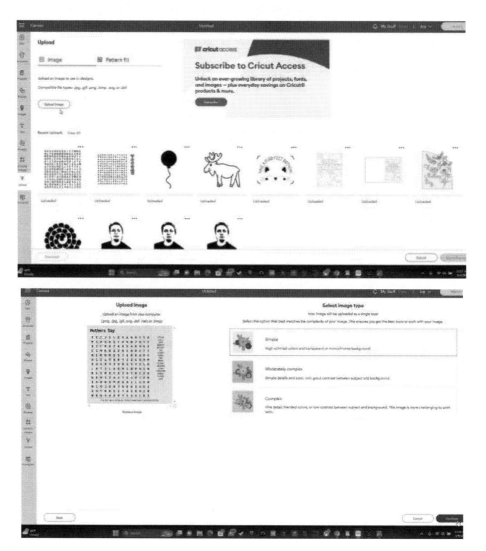

Click 'apply' and 'continue'. Save the image as print and cut and then click upload. I wanted a template where I could see where all the letters are and I am manually going to type all the letters by hand in design space. You need to type them out in columns, going up and down and not across, and then retype the names too.

Note: After uploading your image do not try to delete the white spaces between the letters, it takes forever and the letters come out blurry. Also, do not type the letters across in rows, the letters will not line up right. When you type the letters column by column, the letters end up in the right spot. Go back to a new canvas, click upload, select the file, and click 'add to canvas'.

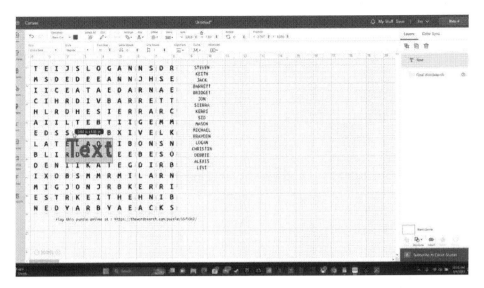

Enlarge the image for better visibility of the letters. Click on "Text," move the text box to the desired location, and begin typing the letters in the correct sequence. To ensure uniform letter size, select a letter and check its size on the top bar. If it shows 0.493, type in 0.5 and press enter. The letter size will now be 0.5 by 0.9656. To align, highlight both columns, click on "Align," and then align them at the top.

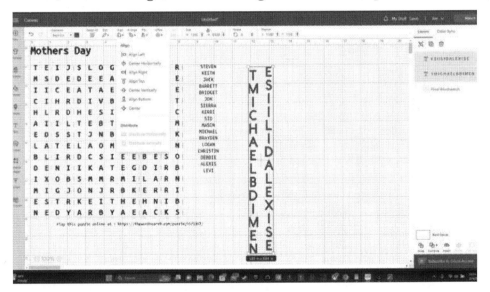

Once you've finished typing all the letters, highlight them all, then click on "Align," choose "Align Top," and finally, click on "Align" again and select "Distribute Horizontally." This will ensure everything aligns perfectly.

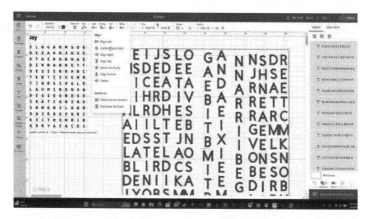

Type in the names too using the same technique.

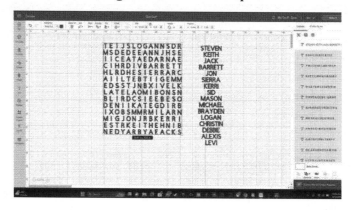

Delete the crossword template, highlight everything, and click 'Combine & Unite'. Go to text, type 'Together' Change the font and to a script font.

To make the letters fancier, use a character map. I want to change the 't' to capital. Using a Windows computer, go to the start bar and type 'character map'. Select it and search for the name of the font you are using. Click 'group by' and go to the Unicode sub-range, still to the bottom of it and select 'private use characters.' You can see all the fancy letters, look for the letter 'r'. Click select and copy it. Go back to your canvas and delete the 'r'. Do control V to paste it.

Click on the text and type ' We are Family' in all capital letters, change the font to a classic one and then click ' weld'.

Take a ruler and measure the size of the erase board to determine how big or small to resize it. The erase board is about 10 inches by 14 inches.

Click on shapes, select a rectangle, tap on the unlock button, change it to 14 inches wide and 10 inches high and change the color to gray. Use the rectangle as a template and delete it later.

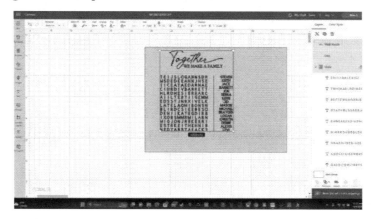

Highlight the entire image and shrink it down to fit into the rectangle. Click 'bring to front'. Delete the rectangle with the eye tool, highlight the entire image, and click 'attach'. Also, highlight all, click 'align', and then 'center horizontally'.

Highlight everything again and click 'Combine & Unite'. Remove the rectangle gray box and click 'Make It'.

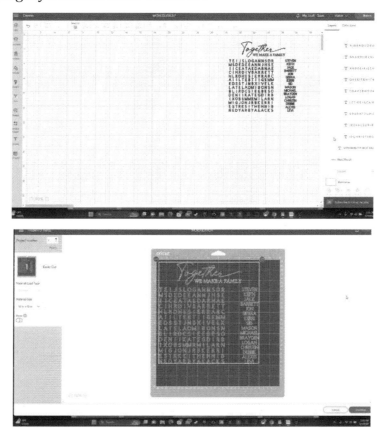

Do not mirror the image because it is not heat travel vinyl, click 'continue'. Set your material - Vinyl. Determine the quantity of vinyl to use by looking at your mat preview. Measure 10 inches of the vinyl and cut it out with the Cricut cutter.

Place the sheet of vinyl in the upper left corner of the Cricut mat and place it into the cutting machine to cut.

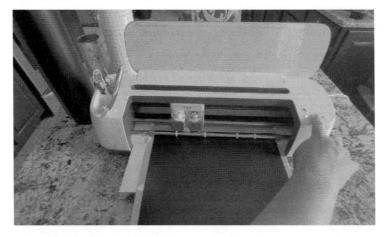

While your design is cutting, dap a little drop of isopropyl into a coffee filter to clean your blank dry-erase board. Allow it to dry.

After cutting, remove your design from the mat by flipping the mat over, holding down your design in one hand and then peeling away the mat with the other hand. Weed your design.

Measure a piece of transfer tape enough to cover your design and press it down with the scraper.

Peel off the backing, leaving the design on the transfer tape.

Flip over your dry-erase board to determine where the mounting bracket is. You don't want to stick the vinyl when the mounting bracket is at the bottom. Carefully line the design on the dry-erase board, and use the grid lines to determine when it is straight.

Press down starting from the center to the outside. Use a scraper to smooth it down, removing all air bubbles.

Gently peel back the transfer tape.

Note: When removing the transfer tape, avoid pulling it straight. Instead, fold it flat back so it's facing your body and lays flat on the dry-erase board. Then, gently pull it towards yourself, wiggling a little bit on both sides as you peel it off.

Your project is complete.

Alphabet Letters Cubes

Materials Needed

- o Cricut Maker or Cricut Explore
- o Cricut Tool Set
- o Cardstock
- o Liquid Adhesive
- o Bone Folder

Instructions

Open a new project in the design space and click on uploads.

Select the two cube letter PNG

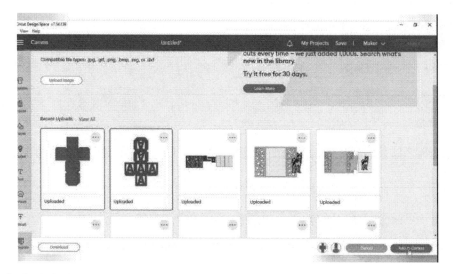

and click 'add to canvas'.

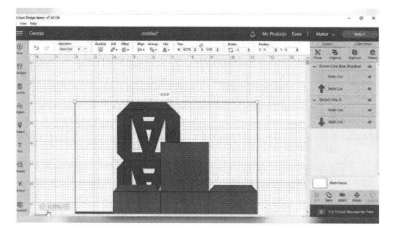

Place both cube structures onto each other to ensure that both will fit perfectly when assembled. Go to the 'ungroup' icon and click 'send to back'.

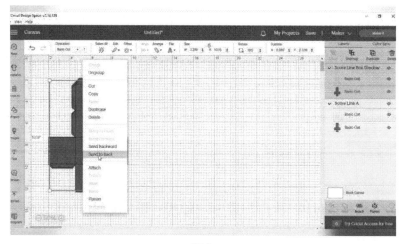

Highlight both cube structures go to the operation icon click on 'basic cut' and then 'score' to add score lines.

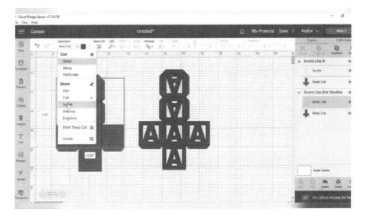

Resize them to be the same size, highlight both structures and stack them on each other by clicking 'bring forward' to ensure they fit well. Detach them and click 'Make It'.

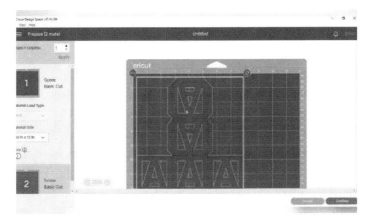

Set your material to light cardstock and set the tool to more pressure.

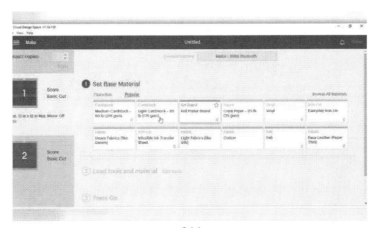

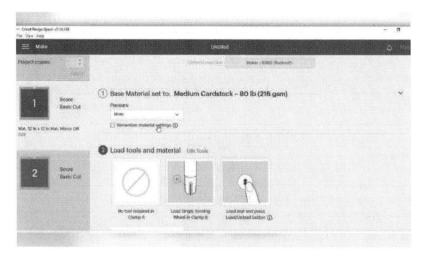

Place the cardstock on a mat and put it in the cutting machine.

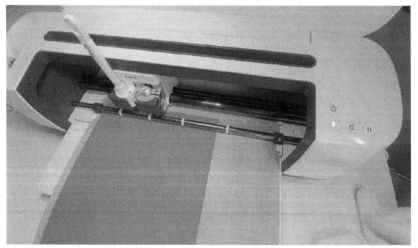

After cutting, peel off the excess cardstock around the mat and remove your design.

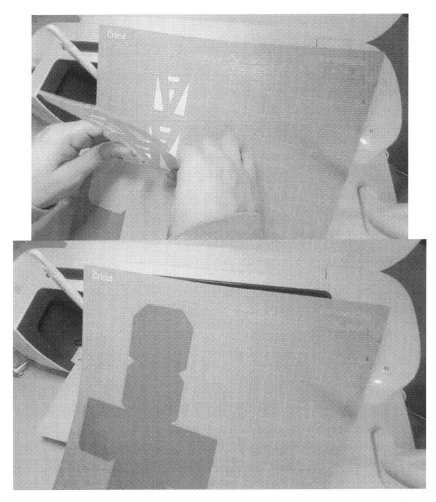

After weeding your design, crease the flaps along the score lines and use a bone folder to achieve a clean, precise fold.

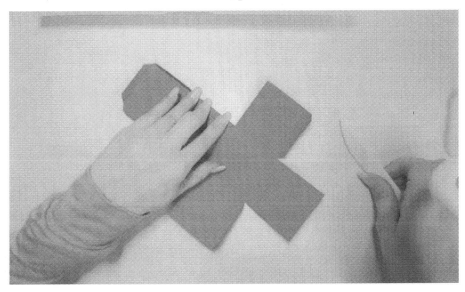

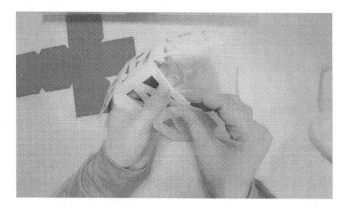

Next, fold the sides to shape the box. Fold the white alphabet letter boxes, apply glue on the flaps to stick them together and leave one side open for attaching the colored boxes later on.

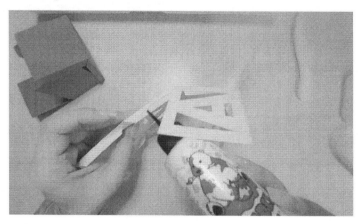

Fold the blue box too.

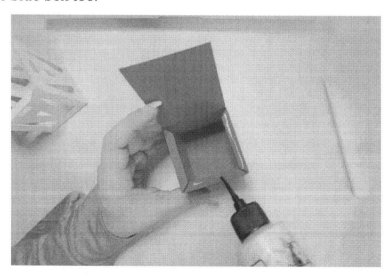

Apply glue on the sides and press down all the sides to form a cube. Insert this cube inside the white alphabet letterbox.

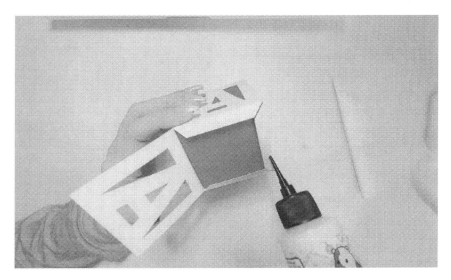

Apply glue on the flaps and press down.

Your alphabet letter box is complete.

Customized Flashcard

Materials Needed

- o Cricut machine
- o Cricut light grip mat
- o Cardstock

o   Printer

o   Weeding tool

Instructions

Open design space and start a new project.

Click the upload button, then select "upload an image" and proceed to upload the PNG file.

Choose 'complex.'

The click 'continue.' Do not remove anything from the background, click 'apply' and 'continue'. Choose 'Print then cut image' and click 'upload'. Select the thumbnail from your recent uploads and then add it to your canvas.

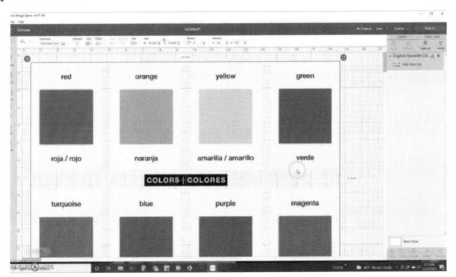

Change the size by going to the size menu and ensure that it is locked so that the proportions stay the same. Change the width to 8.75 the height will automatically change to 6.503.

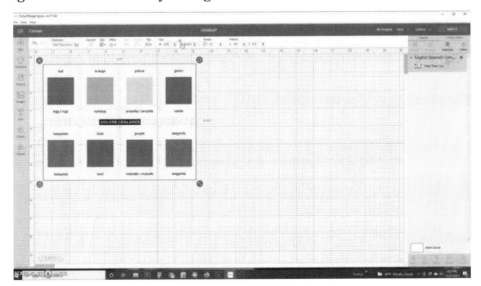

Click 'Make It'. Send the design to your machine and click 'continue'. Click 'send to printer.' Choose the printer that you are going to be using and then click 'print'.

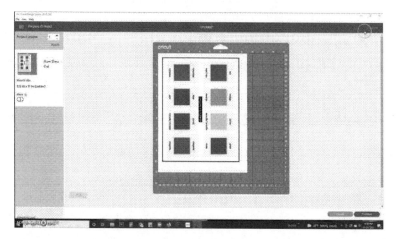

The design will be sent to the printer. Ensure you have the right material loaded in it. Put your printed paper onto your cutting mat and align it exactly as shown in the design space preview window. Set the material type- cardstock by setting the dial to cardstock.

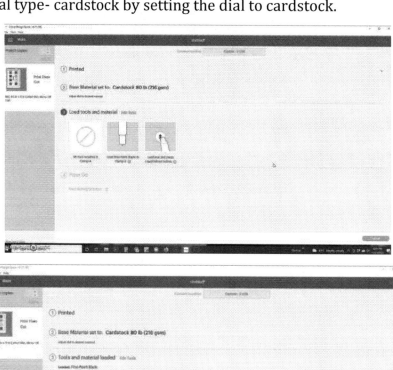

Put it in the cutting machine to cut.

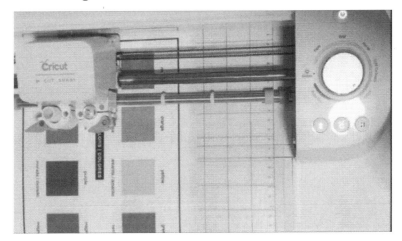

Once the cutting is completed, remove your mat from the machine and weed your cards off of the cutting mat.

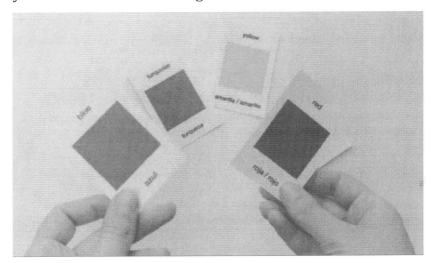

Math Manipulative Sets

Materials Needed for Shape Sensory Bag

- o Cricut machine
- o Cricut strong grip mat
- o Craft foam
- o Scissors
- o Hair gel (1 bottle)

- o Ziplock bags
- o Vinyl
- o Duct tape
- o Craft glue

Instructions.

Open a new project in the Cricut design space. Click on the shape tool and select a triangle, circle, heart, and rectangle. Duplicate the shapes twice, change the colors, and resize to 2 inches by 2 inches.

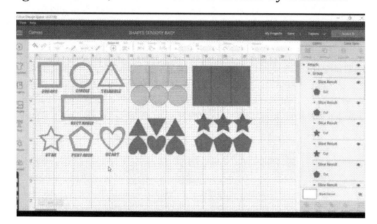

The light blue shapes are the vinyl stickers that will be on the outside of the ziplock bag. The other shapes will be cut out in threes and glued together to make one thick shape that can be pushed around in the hair gel inside the bag. All the shapes have to be exactly 2 inches by 2 inches so that when they push the shapes into the outline of any shape, it will fit inside perfectly.

Click 'Make It'.

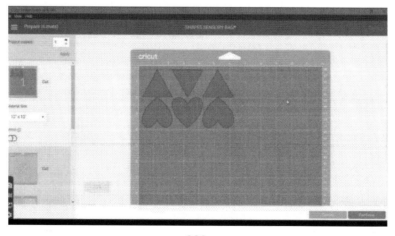

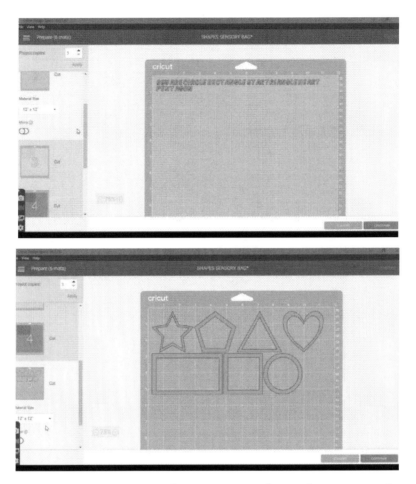

In the preview screen, everything is sorted out for you in the colors that you need. Adjust the design on the mat to ensure that they are in the right spot. Tap on the first mat (orange vinyl) and then click 'continue.' Set the sail of your Cricut Explore 2 to vinyl. Ensure your blade is in the machine.

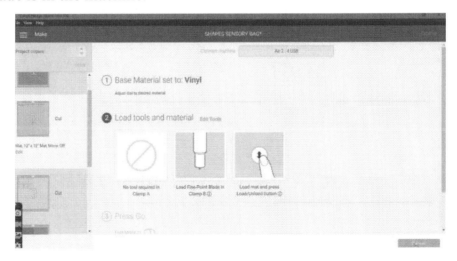

Place the vinyl on the mat and put it in to cut.

Go back to Cricut design space and click 'continue.' Set the dial to craft foam, move the star wheel to the right, and ensure you have not more than 11 inches of base material on the mat. Place the craft foam on cutting the mat and put it in to cut.

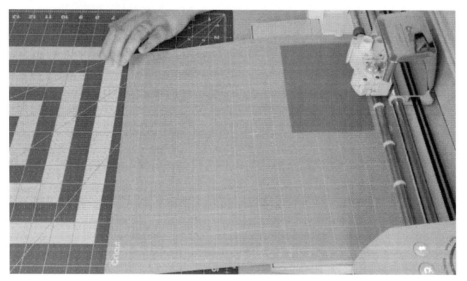

Repeat this process for the remaining shapes in the designated colors and cut.

After cutting, remove the mat from the machine and take your design off the mat.

Weed your design.

Place all the vinyl outline shapes in one ziplock bag. The side that has the white spot will go on the bottom so that the stickers will go on the front side of the bag. Line up the sticks in front of the bag the way it is in the design space.

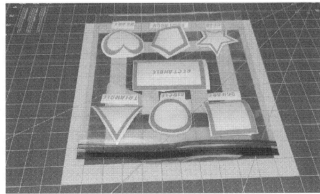

Remove the white backing, place the design on the ziplock bag, press it down and then peel off the transfer tape.

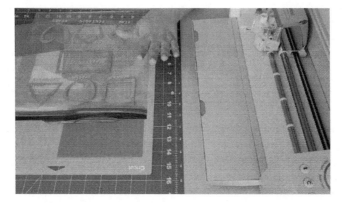

Repeat this step for all the vinyl outline shapes. Glue together all the shapes of the same color to form one large shape. Set aside the bag containing the stickers on one side. Then, take another ziplock bag and pour a full bottle of hair gel into it.

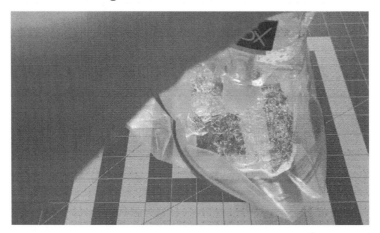

Spread it out inside the bag and throw the foam shapes inside it.

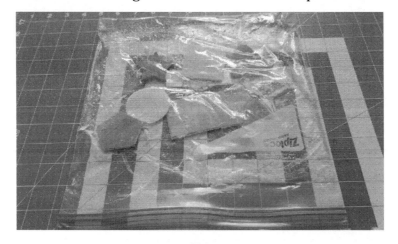

Put the ziplock bag with the gel and foam shapes with the zipper side on the bottom into the ziplock with the outline stickers.

Wrap duct tape around all four edges to provide protection in case the bag pops at the corners.

Here is the completed shape sensory bag.

Chapter 14

Travel and Adventure

Customized Travel Mugs

Materials Needed

- o Cricut machine
- o Cricut light grip mat
- o Weeding tool
- o Scraper
- o Transfer tape
- o Removable vinyl
- o Cricut cutter
- o Scissors
- o Travel mug
- o Isopropyl
- o Towel

Instructions

Measure the surface area of the mug to know how large the decal will be.

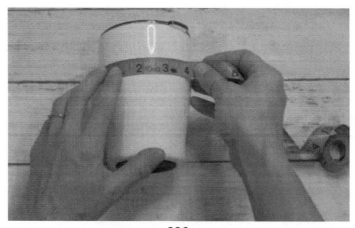

On a new canvas in the design space, click on the text tool and type 'Blondie next door.'

Tap on the font at the top menu and choose a font. Reduce the spacing between the letters by clicking on the letter spacing icon. Highlight the text, click the unlock button and resize the text to fit perfectly on the mug manually by typing in the number. Click 'Attach' and then 'Weld.' When you are done, tap 'Make It'. In the preview screen, mirror your text and click 'continue'

Set your base material to Removable Vinyl. Ensure the blade is correctly placed in your Cricut.

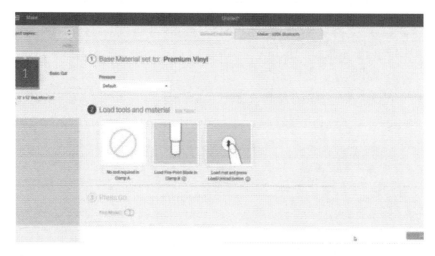

Place the vinyl on the mat and insert it in the cutting machine.

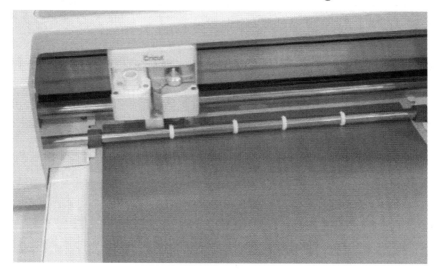

After cutting, peel your design from the mat by lifting the mat away from the design. Trim the vinyl as close as possible to the word and weed out your design.

Cut a piece of transfer tape large enough to cover your design, then place it on top of the design. Press it down with the scraper, and peel off your design. Make small snips at the top and bottom of the design for easier application using scissors. Dampen a lint-free towel with isopropyl alcohol and clean the surface of the mug. Finally, apply the design onto the mug.

Press it down with a scraper.

Peel off the transfer tape leaving your design on the mug.

Repeat the same steps with the other design.

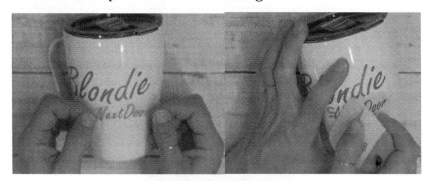

Your project is complete.

Personalized Travel Journals

Material Needed

- o   Cricut machine
- o   Cricut knife blade + drive housing

- Cricut strong grip mat
- Cricut standard grip mat
- Cricut scoring wheel
- Bone folder
- Cricut brayer
- Scissors
- Masking tape
- Cricut leather metallic rose gold
- 12 inches × 12 inches cardstock
- ¼ inched Ribbon
- Lip roller
- Cardstock

Instructions

Open the design space and click on the projects. This journal caught my attention and it is the same project that is featured on their leather packaging. This project has a rundown of the materials and directions on how to assemble it.

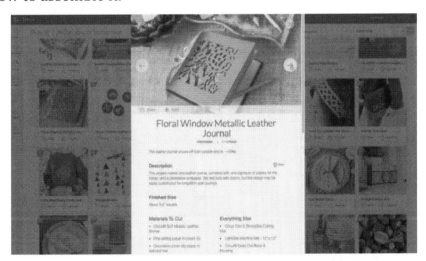

Preview the project to see the actual measurements and look at all the files.

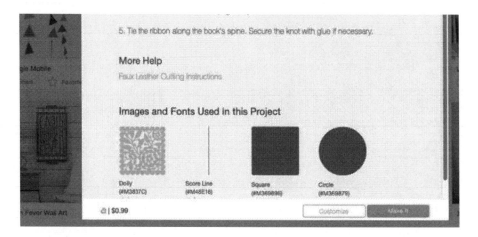

The main benefit of this project is that it's all laid out.

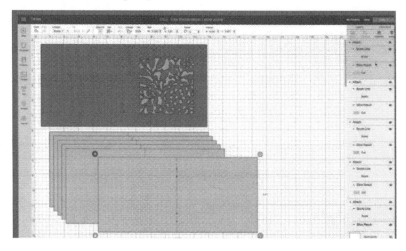

Click 'Make It'.

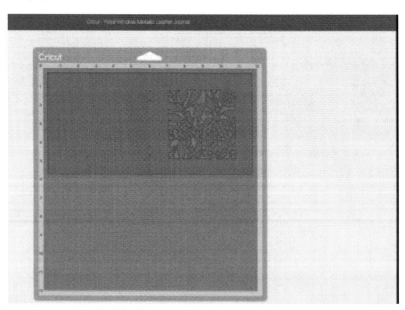

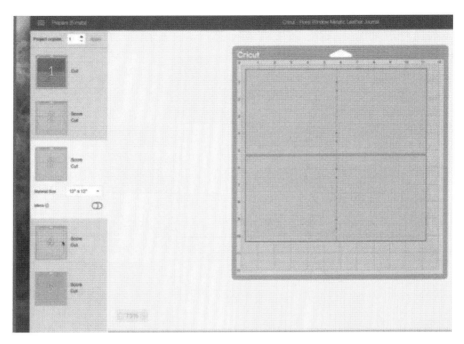

Arrange your materials on the mat and feed them through the machine. Follow the steps outlined on the left-hand side of the design space, beginning with the cover. Position the metallic rose gold leather on a strong grip mat, ensuring the smooth side is facing down. Use a brayer to flatten it, then secure all four sides with masking tape. Return to the design space, toggle the mirror icon, and proceed by clicking 'continue.' Access the settings, select 'browse all materials,' and opt for metallic rose leather.

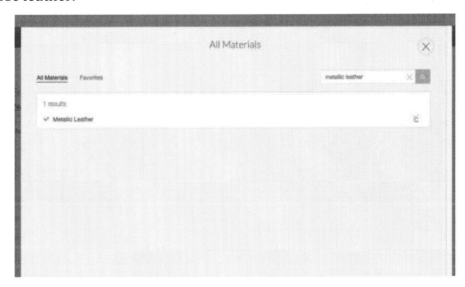

Set your tools too- knife blade.

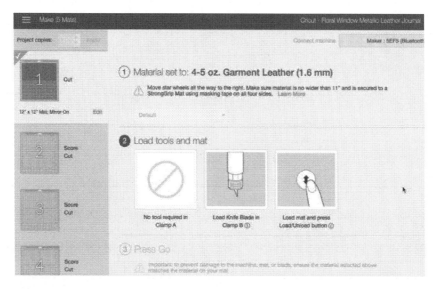

Push all the star wheels to one side so it doesn't dent the leather.

After cutting, remove all the negative spaces from the design and clean up the inside with a blip roller.

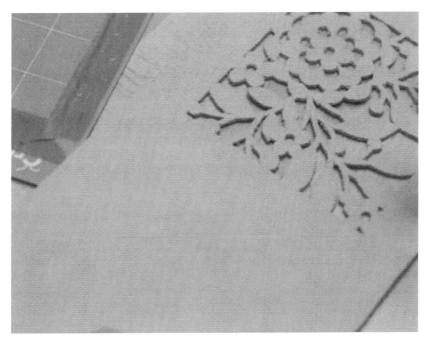

For the pages, use four 12" by 12" cardstock. Stick it on a standard grip mat, go back to design space and select the weight of the cardstock you are using.

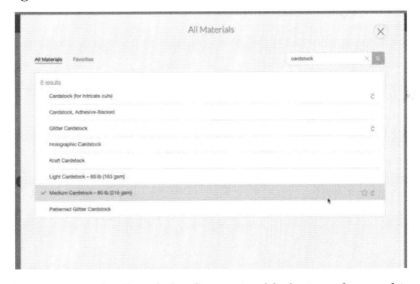

Place the scoring wheel and the fine point blade into the machine then place the mat into the cutting machine.

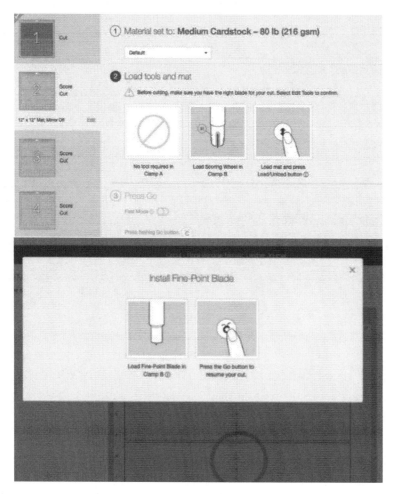

It will score the lines in the middle of the pages making it easier to fold and the knife blade will cut the pages.

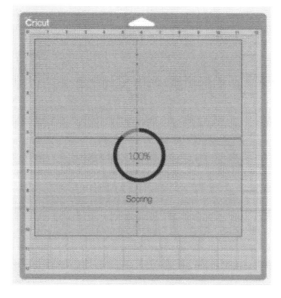

After cutting, reverse the mat onto your tabletop and hold the cardstock while bending the mat.

Repeat this process for the remaining pages.

Stack all the papers together, since they are scored, it should make it easier to fold them centered making one big signature.

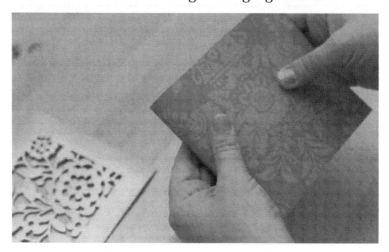

To bind them with the cover, use ¼ inch wide ribbon and single thread it into an embroidery needle. Starting from the outside, leave a long piece on the outside so that it will be part of the bow, returning it to the next set of holes depending on the thickness of your ribbon and cardstock.

You may need to navigate through each page individually, threading the needle through each one towards the inside. When you reach the last hole, which should be on the outside of the book, tie a knot with the two pieces of thread, followed by a bow on top.

 Trim any excess with the Cricut cutter and then fold it all together in the page measurement that was in the project file.

DIY Map Art

Materials Needed

- o Cricut machine
- o Cricut standard grip mat
- o Circular wood piece
- o Removable adhesive vinyl (white)
- o Standard grip transfer tape
- o Weeding tool

- Scraper
- Electric sander
- Abrasive paper
- Fabric
- Wood stain
- Water-based polyacrylic.
- Painter's tape
- Level
- Resin
- Mixing cup
- Plastic drop cloth
- Mixing stick
- Trowel
- Heat gun
- Butane torch.

Instructions

Purchase or create a circular wood piece with a diameter of 17.75 inches.

Smoothly sand the front, back, and sides of the wood round. Eliminate sanding residue by wiping the wood with a cloth.

Apply your selected wood stain to the front, sides, and back of the wood round. Allow the stain to dry thoroughly and cure for a full 24-hour period. Then, coat the front and sides of your wood round with a thin layer of water-based polycrylic.

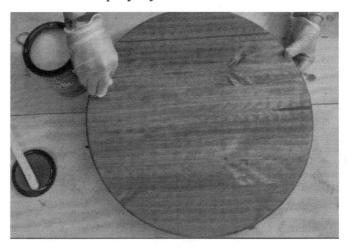

Be mindful of drips on the underside. Adhere to the recoating times specified in your sealer instructions. Apply three layers, waiting 2 hours between each, and sand with 220-grit sandpaper before the final layer. Allow the Polycrylic to cure for a full 24 hours before proceeding to the resin seal coat. Once the Polycrylic has fully cured, apply the resin seal coat. This step is crucial to prevent the occurrence of tiny bubbles in the resin when poured onto wood. The seal coat, a thin layer of resin, serves to prevent these bubbles from forming underneath the vinyl. Secure the edges on the underside of your wood round with painter's tape to catch drips and ensure a clean underside for your project.

Precision is crucial; avoid tape protruding from underneath to prevent unsightly ridges during resin pouring. Identify a suitable pouring location, considering the temperature sensitivity of your resin, and lay a plastic drop cloth to protect the surface. Elevate and level your project on the pouring surface, checking for levelness from various directions.

Follow the resin mixing instructions specific to your brand. Apply a thin layer of resin and enhance viscosity by using a heat gun. Use a trowel to spread the resin, ensuring comprehensive coverage of all edges without leaving any bare spots. Use the torch to eliminate emerging bubbles.

Carefully monitor the project for the initial 30-45 minutes to address any bubble issues. Cover the project and allow the resin to fully cure; for the ProMarine resin, a duration of three full days was observed. Obtain a world map illustration to suit your preferences. My specific choice was made through Alamy.com.

Make sure the graphic is compatible with your cutting machine's capacity; if needed, segment the graphic according to the size of your wood round. In this process, I used Photoshop to divide the selected world map into three pieces.

Save the images in PNG format to maintain a transparent background. Upload the graphics into the Design Space.

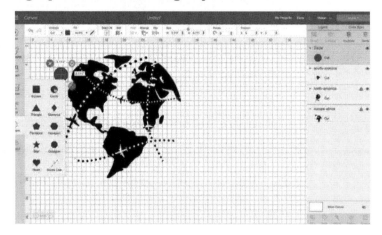

Select a circle in the shape tool, resize it to the size of the round wood, and change the color to blue. Place the map inside the circle.

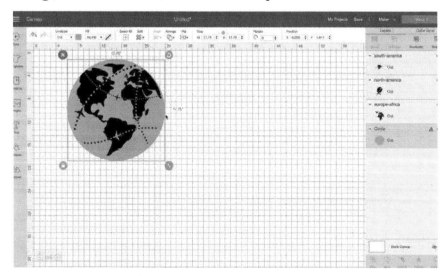

Adjust the size of the graphics as required to align with the dimensions of your wood round. When you are done, delete the blue circle and click 'Make It'.

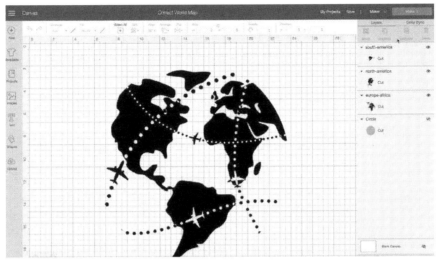

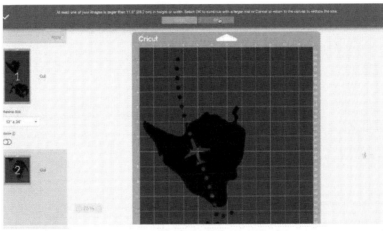

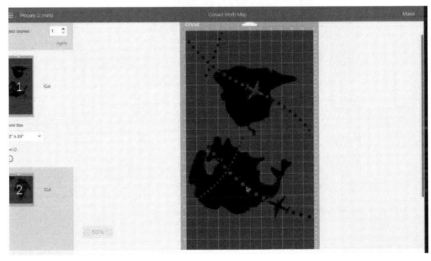

Set the material to premium vinyl and ensure the blade is in the machine.

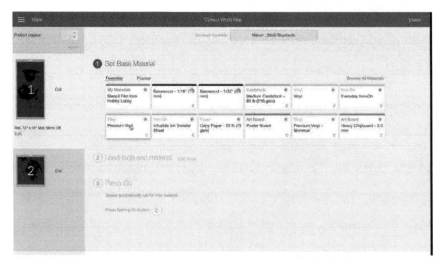

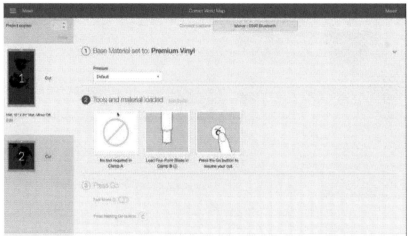

Place the vinyl on the mat and put it in the cutting machine.

After cutting, weed out the excess vinyl.

Connect graphics with connecting lines, such as flight paths in our example, before attempting the application.

Securely tape the graphics with double-sided tape on the back of the backing paper to prevent movement during the transfer tape application.

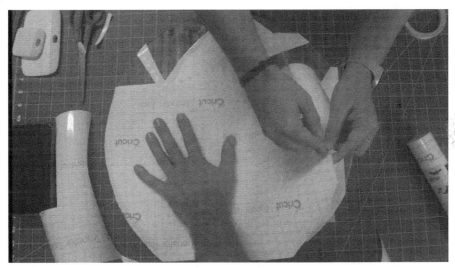

Apply transfer tape to the top of the vinyl graphic, ensuring a smooth, bubble-free surface. Once the transfer tape completely covers the graphic, position it onto your sealed wood round. Ensure precise alignment by adjusting the placement until all edges match. While keeping the entire graphic in position, lift one corner, peel off the vinyl backing, and affix the adhesive graphic with transfer tape onto the board.

Continue lifting the graphic, pressing it carefully into place using a scraper on the transfer tape's front, and gradually peeling back the backing.

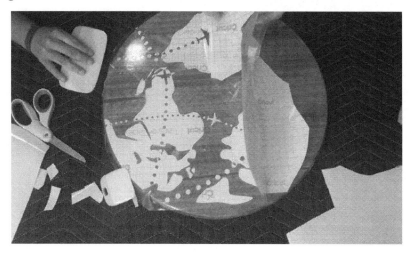

After fully adhering the design, slowly peel off the transfer tape. Address any bubbles by puncturing them with a pin and pressing them down. Allow the vinyl to set for 24 hours before progressing to the resin flood coat. Follow the resin mixing instructions specific to your brand. Pour a dense resin layer and heat it with a heat gun for added viscosity. Gently spread the resin with a trowel, being cautious not to lift any edges of the vinyl graphic. Ensure comprehensive coverage of all edges, avoiding bare spots. Use a torch to eliminate bubbles as they arise. Cover and allow the resin to cure completely; in our case with ProMarine resin, we allotted three full days. Carefully remove the tape from the bottom after the resin has cured, and if necessary, delicately break any persistent seals between the resin and the tape using a box cutter.

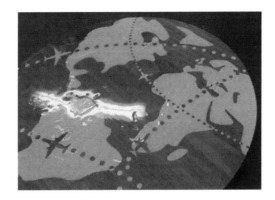

Vacation Memory Albums

Materials Needed

- o Cricut machine
- o Cricut standard grip mat
- o Cardstock
- o String
- o Scissors
- o Sticky tape
- o Scallop circle punch

Instructions

Open the design space and click on 'all categories.' Scroll down to where it says 'Photo memories.'

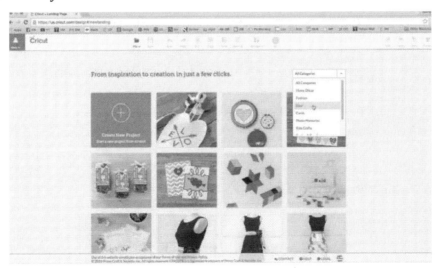

Click on the "Vacation Mini Album" to open the preview window. At the bottom, you'll find a price tag.

Cricut requires payment for certain shapes. To avoid this, create your shapes so you can cut the mini album for free. Click on "customize" to view the shapes they intend to charge you for — the banner pieces and some 1-inch circles.

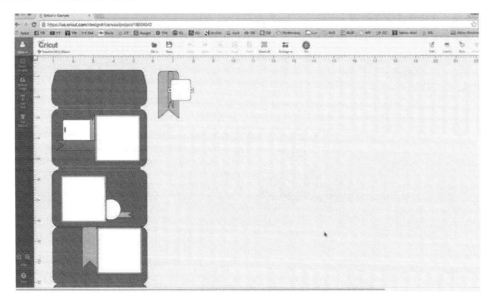

On the left-hand side of the bar, click on 'insert image' in the search box and type the word 'banner'. Select a banner.

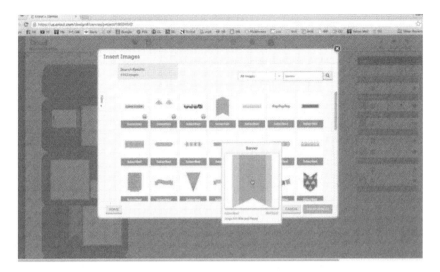

Type 'circles' select a circle and click on 'insert images'.

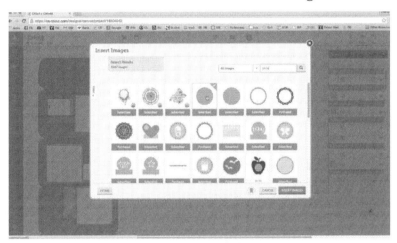

Shift the circle to one side. The banner consists of two layers. Select the banner, right-click, and choose "ungroup" to remove the layer you don't need.

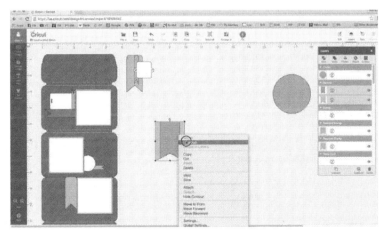

351

There are a lot of banners on this project, go to the top toolbar click 'copy' and then paste. Do this three times to have four banners. Use your mouse to hover over the four banners, click copy and then paste again. Making it a total of eight banner pieces.

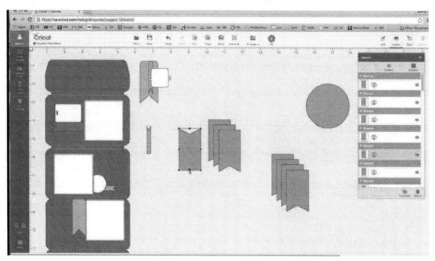

Remove the paid banners from the project and substitute them with a free banner. Select the spinner and press the shift key while clicking the keyboard and the outer circle. When hovering over it, you'll notice two small arrows that enable rotation. Holding down the shift button keeps it straight.

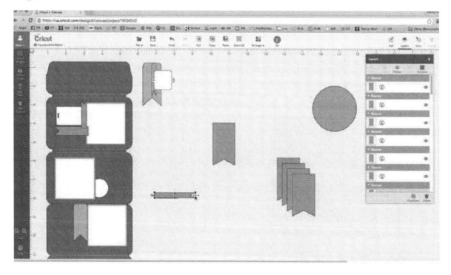

Take a banner and line it up to the side, use the handle on the outside to make it roughly the same as the one below it. Do the same step for all eight banners. Delete the paid banners and insert your design into the project. Click on the square, right-click, and then tap 'ungroup' to remove the second layer.

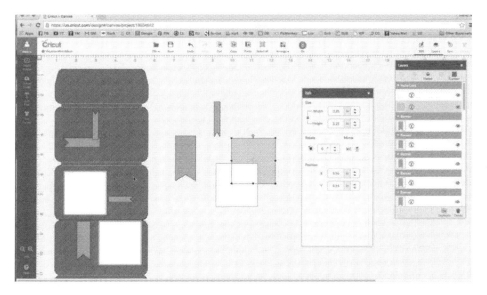

The photo mask is layered, go to edit, click on it, and tap 'ungroup.' I will use white cardstock and a background color which is the photo mat. The larger one is the background and is 2.25 inches by 2.25 inches. I will cut six 2" by 2" squares from cardstock. Select any other elements you won't need for this project.

Click 'Make It'.

The book is on one mat at 8" by 11" and on another mat are all the banner pieces. You can decide to cut them with one color or put them at different points with different colors of the cardstock.

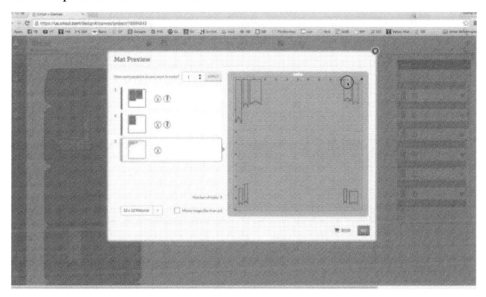

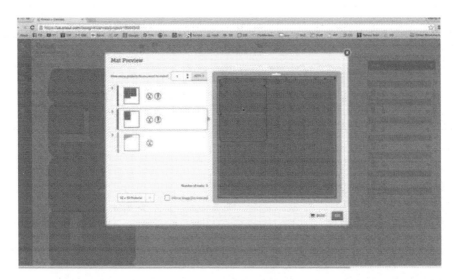

Set your materials - cardstock and tools. Place the cardstock on the mat and place it in the cutting machine. After cutting, assemble the mini album. Fold in all the score lines for the book creasing with a bone folder.

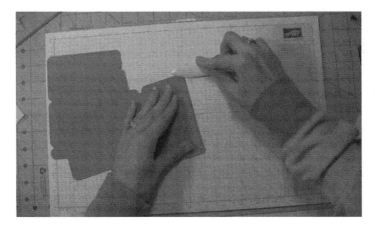

Place score tape on the flaps of the album and place them so they overlap, adhering well.

Place your photo mat one on each using the sticky tape to glue it down. Add the banners too. Use two different background stamps to put designs on the album.

Fold the album in accordion style and clip the front to the hook. Glue a larger banner on the front.

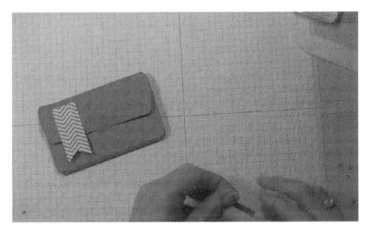

Take some twine and wrap it around the front, knot it and make a bow. Use the sticky tape and paste a circle on top of the twine to hold it down. Place a love sticker on top of the small circle to complete the project.

Chapter 15

DIY Gifts

Customized Glassware Sets

Material Needed

o Cricut machine

o Permanent vinyl

o Libbey can glasses

o Scraper

o Wedding tool

o Scissors

o Coffee filter paper

o Rubbing alcohol

o Transfer tape

Instruction

Prepare each glass by wiping it with rubbing alcohol on a coffee filter paper to prevent dirt or lint from affecting the vinyl transfer. Open the design space and create a new canvas. Click on templates and choose patterns. Select the shape tool, pick a square, and resize it to 9.25 x 4.25 inches. Change the color to white. This will serve as a template.

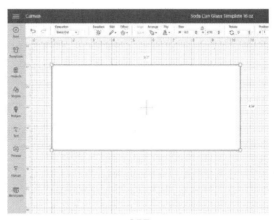

Insert the images into 'Design Space Canvas' and adjust their size to match the template.

Click 'Make It.' Set your material - permanent Vinyl and your tools. Place the vinyl into the Cricut to cut. After cutting, weed your design. Cut a piece of transfer tape, place it onto your design, and press it down with a scraper. Peel back the design. Position it on the glassware, press it down with a scraper, and peel back the transfer tape, leaving your design on the glassware. Repeat this same step for the remaining designs.

Personalized Cutting Boards

Materials Needed

- o Cutting Board
- o Wood Burning Marker
- o Cricut

- o   Etsy Monogram File

- o   Vinyl

- o   Transfer Tape

- o   Weeding Tools

- o   220 Sanding Sponge

- o   Heat Gun

- o   Cutting Board Oil or Mineral Oil

- o   Paper Towels

- o   Cricut BrightPad (optional)

Instructions

Open a new canvas in the Cricut Design Space. Click on "Images" and then "Image Sets." Type "Motifs" in the search bar. Look for the letter "W" and choose the dark blue version. Click "Add to Canvas."

To split the letter "W," select "Shapes" and choose a rectangle. Unlock its proportions and adjust the width to match the letter. Set the height to 0.25 inches and position it slightly above the center of the letter. Select both shapes, align them, and center them horizontally. Slice the shapes to remove the unwanted portion. Now, the design is split but still in one piece, so it needs to be separated into two pieces to add the text "waters."

Go back to "Shapes" and select another rectangle. Place it in the bottom half of the letter, ensuring it's centered. Select both shapes and slice them. Remove the excess and delete it. Your monogram is now in two separate pieces.

To add bars across to frame the halves of the monogram, choose "Shapes" again and select a rectangle. Adjust its width to match the letter and set the height to 0.25 inches. Place it along the edge of the top half, then select both shapes, align them, and center them horizontally. Duplicate the first bar, align it with the bottom half, select both bottom pieces, and click "Weld."

Now, add text by clicking on the text icon, typing "waters" in the center and changing the font. Place the text inside the "W," select all, align them, and center them horizontally. Finally, resize the image to fit on the cutting board.

When you are done, select all and click 'attach'. Click 'Make It'. Review the mat screen. Set your material - vinyl, ensure the tool is set properly and set it to more pressure. Place your vinyl on the mat and put it in the Cricut to cut.

Use a weeding tool to weed the design. As the vinyl functions as a stencil, focus on eliminating the positive elements of the design (including text) while retaining the negative aspects. Apply transfer tape over the vinyl stencil's surface.

Sand the cutting board with 220 grit sandpaper for a smoother surface.

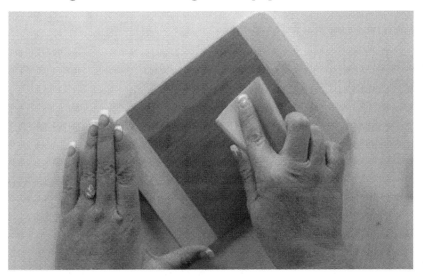

A smoother surface reduces the risk of ink bleeding when coloring with the marker. Position the vinyl stencil on the cutting board as desired.

Gently peel off the transfer tape, pressing the vinyl onto the wood with the scraper tool and your finger to ensure adhesion and eliminate bubbles. Have a paper towel ready as you fill in the stencil with a wood-burning marker.

Periodically dab the marker's tip on the paper towel to avoid excess ink and potential bleeding in the design. You can also blot the paper towel on the wood's surface to absorb any extra ink.

The marker ink might be subtle, especially on certain wood tones; refrain from adding more ink in an attempt to enhance visibility. Set the heat gun to 1000°F. Keep the vinyl stencil on the board and evenly apply heat to the inked design.

Avoid applying heat outside the stencil area; focus on revealing the burn inside the marked section.

When warm, promptly use a weeding tool to peel off the vinyl stencil. Delaying may cause sticky residue due to heating.

To safeguard the board, use a paper towel, rag, or cotton ball to apply 'Cutting Board Oil.'

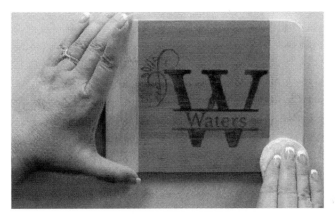

Allow the cutting board to air dry for at least an hour.

Handmade Candles with Unique Labels

Materials needed

- o Cricut machine
- o Cricut blue light grip mat
- o Candle jar
- o Printable vinyl
- o Inkjet printer
- o Ruler

Instructions.

Measure the jar to determine how big you want the label to be. You may want the label to wrap around the jar. We are going to do a 4.5 inches by 2.75 inches.

Open a new canvas in the Cricut design space, click on the shape tool and select a rectangle. Resize the rectangle to the dimension of the jar. Click the unlock button on the top menu, and type in 2.75 high and 4.50 width. Change the color of the rectangle to white and add a photo.

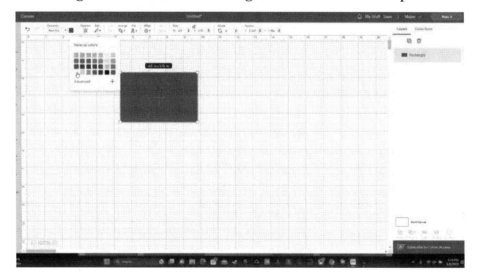

To upload a photo, go to upload an image, browse, and then select a file that you have saved on your computer. Select 'complex', click 'apply' and 'continue'. Select 'Print then cut image' and then click Upload.

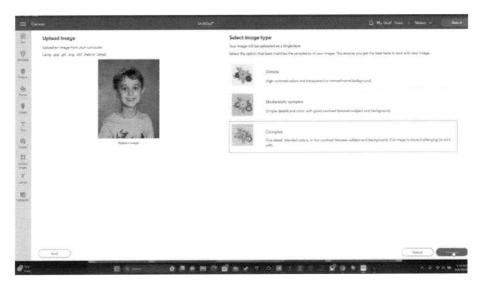

Select the photo and click 'Apply to Canvas.' I want the photo to be the same height as the rectangle. Click 2.75 but do not unlock it. I want the picture to stay proportional, drag it over. You can see the rectangle has curved edges, slice this photo to fit into the curved edges.

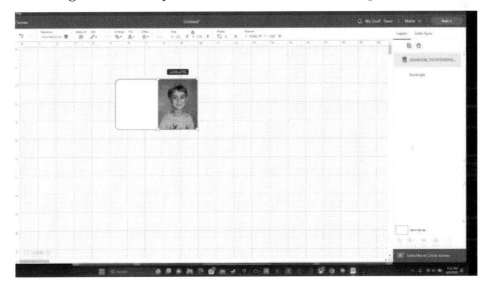

Right-click and tap 'Bring forward'. Click the photo in the back, select the shift button, and then select the rectangle. This makes the slice button available to click. I can click 'slice' and delete this piece.

365

Highlight the entire design, click 'align' and then 'align at the top'.

To add some words to the design, click the text, type 'Thank you for' and select a font. Shrink the size down. The letters are spaced far away from one another, to shrink the spacings, go to the letter spacing icon and tap on the down arrow until the letters get closer to where you would like them to be.

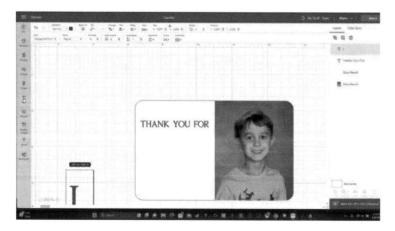

Click text and type 'lighting', change the font, and move it over here.

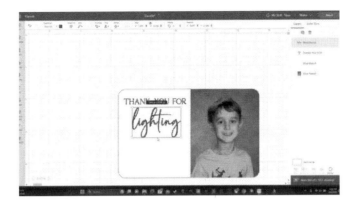

Click text again and type 'up my life'. Duplicate this so that it will be about the same size when you retype.

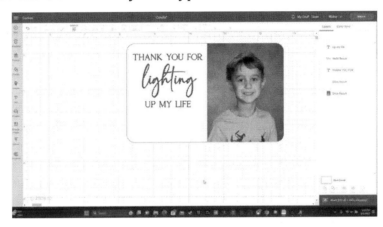

Next, click on text and type 'love Barrett' change to a script font, resize and arrange the design.

Highlight the whole design and click 'flatten.' Now, it's all one piece and I should be able to print it out on my printer. Click 'Make It'. Set up as a 'Print and then cut.

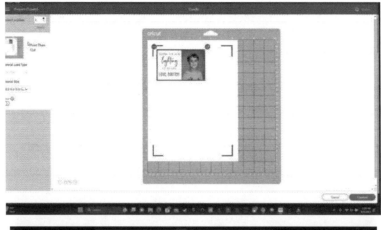

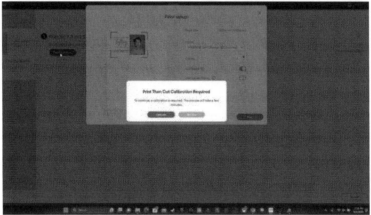

Click 'continue,' send it to the printer, and print.

Stick your printed paper on the upper left-hand corner of the mat and smooth it down flat. Select your material - printable vinyl and click done.

Place the mat in the Cricut to cut.

Dip a piece of coffee filter into isopropyl to clean the surface of the blank jar. Wait for a few minutes to dry up before applying the vinyl. Measure the jar to determine where to place the sticker. Place the sticker on the jar and smooth it down.

DIY Memory Quilts

Materials Needed

- Cricut marker
- Cricut fabric cutting mat
- Cricut Rotary blade
- Self-healing mat
- Rotary cutter
- Acrylic ruler
- Fabric. 35- 10x10" blocks of fabric for the front, 35- 10x10" (Riley BlakeQuilter's cotton) blocks for the back, and 35 blocks of 8x8" for the interior. (Minky)
- Sewing Machine
- Multi-color threads
- Scissors
- Wonder clips or pins
- Fabric spray adhesive

Instructions

Open a new canvas in the design space, click on shapes, select a square, tap on the size icon at the top menu, and unlock the button. Resize the square to 8" × 8". Click 'duplicate' to the required number of quilt blocks.

Click on shapes again, select a square and reduce to 10" × 10", change the color, and duplicate to the required number of quilt blocks.

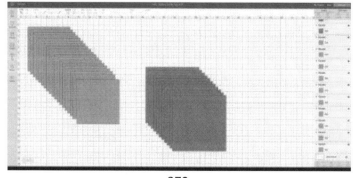

Use a rotary cutter and acrylic to trim your fabric and batting into lengthy strips, ensuring they are slightly wider than the intended final width. As an illustration, I cut my batting to a width of 9 inches.

Click 'Make It' located in the upper right corner of your screen within Cricut Design Space. Select your machine and indicate the fabric type for cutting. Load the cutting mat with fabric, insert your rotary cutter, load the mats into your machine, and initiate the cutting process.

Use elongated fabric strips, allowing the surplus to hang off the cutting mat's edge. After cutting the initial set of blocks on the mat, I shifted the fabric upwards, reloading it into the Maker to proceed with cutting the subsequent blocks.

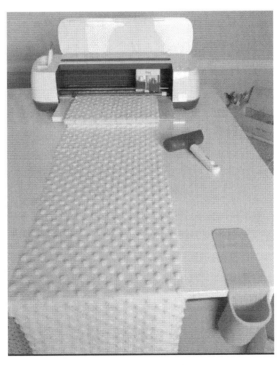

Begin by gathering each quilt block component. Stack a backing square (such as a minky), a centered batting square with a 1-inch border and a top fabric layer (like Riley Blake quilter's cotton). To prevent shifting during sewing, apply fabric spray adhesive inside each quilt block sandwich.

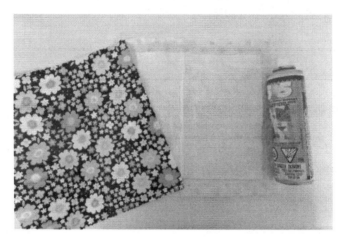

Proceed by sewing an X on every quilt block. Begin from one corner, sewing a straight line down and across to the opposite corner. Repeat the process on the opposite side for all quilt block sandwiches.

After sewing all quilt block sandwiches together, lay out the quilt to determine the desired assembly. Once satisfied with the layout, organize each row into a stack and assign numerical labels to indicate their order. Then, stitch your quilt blocks together to form each row. Begin by grabbing the initial two squares from your first-row stack, ensuring the desired front fabric is facing out and the minky backing is facing in. Sew along the chosen edge, using a 1-inch seam allowance, to join the two quilt blocks together.

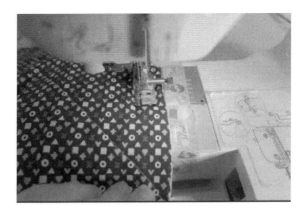

Continue the procedure by adding each quilt block to the row, repeating the process until you complete the first row of your quilt. Set aside the finished row and replicate the steps for each subsequent row in your quilt.

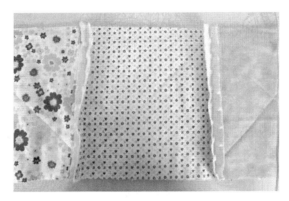

Place your initial two rows on top of each other, aligning the front fabric outward and the minky backing inward. Align and nest the seams, then secure them in place using wonder clips or pins.

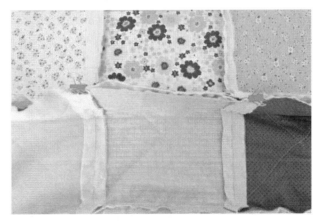

Sew along the edge to join the rows, maintaining a 1-inch seam allowance. Repeat this process for each row of your quilt.

Complete the quilt by finishing the edges. Do a 1-inch seam allowance and sew around all four sides of your blanket, opting for either a straight stitch or a zigzag stitch.

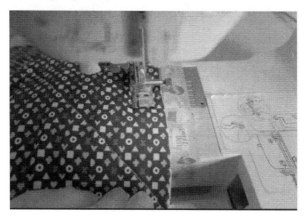

Start by using scissors to make snips every 1/4 to 1/2 inch along the entire outer edge of your blanket and on each exposed seam. Make sure to cut through both the quilting cotton and the Minky, being careful to only cut the fabric and not the stitches.

Once you've completed the snipping process, toss your rag quilt into the washer and dryer. This step promotes fraying along the seams and enhances the quilt's softness, making it extra cozy.

Enjoy your exquisite DIY rag quilt! Whether keeping it for cozy moments on the couch or presenting it as a lovely handmade gift, your creation is sure to bring warmth and comfort.

Customized Gift Boxes

Materials Needed

- o   Cricut machine
- o   Cricut standard grip mat
- o   Permanent running tape

- o Cardstock
- o Scoring stylus
- o Scissors
- o Fine point blade

Instructions

Go to Google and type templatemaker.nl, a website offering an extensive array of customizable Cricut box templates available for download. A glance at the front page reveals a diverse range of options to choose from.

Choose any template from the top menu, and it will open for customization. You can use millimeters, centimeters, or inches to input the specific dimensions needed. Ensure that your design is compatible with your Cricut machine by selecting an appropriate paper size. Pull down the page size box and choose either 12 x 24 or 24 x 12 inches based on the orientation, making sure it fits on your selected paper.

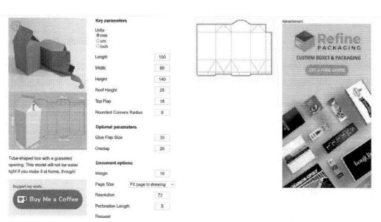

Keep adding dimensions until you reach the desired size that fits within the paper dimensions you've chosen. For optimal exporting, click "Cricut," then choose 'Create' to download your file. While the SVG button works, it might import excessively large into Cricut Design Space, making resizing difficult. I suggest using the Cricut button for better results.

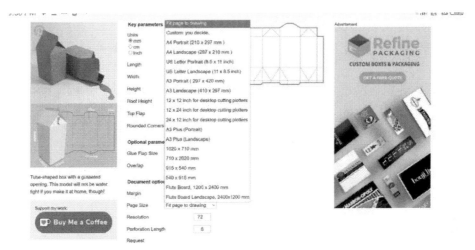

After downloading the template, upload the file to Cricut Design Space. Although all content is imported as cut lines, most of it should be marked as score lines. In this case, there are three distinct groups. You can minimize each group by clicking the arrow next to it. Select the top group and then click 'ungroup.'

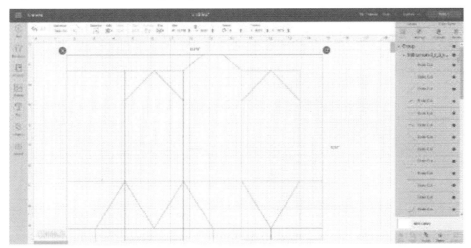

Next, examine each of the remaining groups and identify which lines should be marked as score lines, usually those on the inside. To do this, select the second group and click on 'score.'

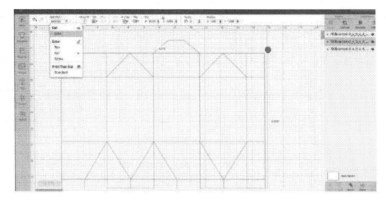

Repeat the process for any other groups requiring score lines, using solid lines for cuts and dashed lines for scoring.

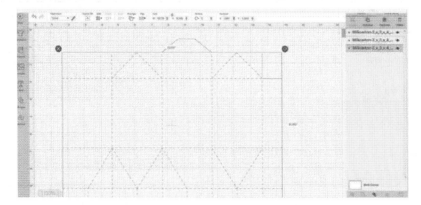

Select all elements and choose "attach." Adjust the size to fit the paper if needed. Click 'Make it' and the entire design should be visible on one mat.

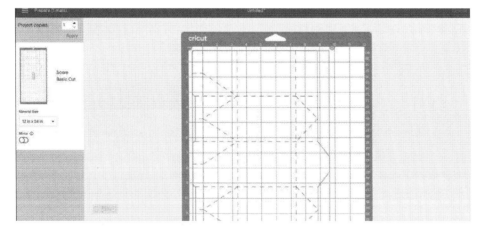

Select the material for the project- cardstock and set your tools - scoring stylus & fine point blade. Place the cardstock on a standard grip mat and put it in the Cricut to score and cut.

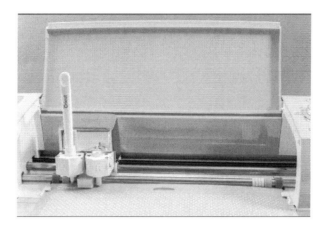

Fold along the score lines and apply glue to the areas where overlaps occur.

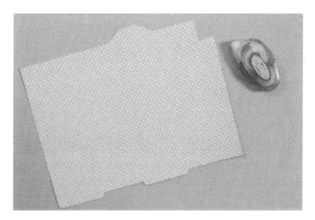

Use a permanent tape runner, apply it along the glue flaps, and then assemble the paper box.

Note that the top should not be glued; simply fold it in after placing your gift inside.

379

Chapter 16

Personalized Home Accents

Decorated Throw Pillow Covers

Materials Needed

- o Pillow cover (18 × 18 inches)
- o Cricut machine
- o Cricut standard grip mat
- o Heat transfer vinyl
- o Cricut easy press
- o Weeding tool
- o Easy press mat
- o Lint roller
- o Teflon sheet

Instructions

Open a new canvas in the Cricut design space, go to images, and type 'Fall'. Go to ownership and click 'free'. There are only seven results for the search. Click on the design and then tap Insert Images

Go to the layer panel and click ungroup. To change all the individual elements in this design to black, use the color sync button. Select everything, click on the color sync, and move each piece that is not black up to the black.

The acorn's top piece is not connected to the bottom pieces, to adjust it go to the layer panel and turn off everything that is not part of the acorn. Click on shapes and select a square. I'm going to slice out the acorn so that I can get it how I want it. Resize the square, place it on top of the acorn, and rotate it. Ensure that the square covers the bottom part of the acorn. Select everything including the square and click slice.

Delete the gray piece. Turn off everything that is not part of the acorn. Click on shapes again and select a square. Resize it to fit on top of the upper part of the acorn. Select everything and click slice. Delete the gray pieces.

Hide the welcome piece, turn back on the acorn, and turn back on the bottom part of the acorn. Place the top and bottom piece of acorn close the way you want it. Go to shapes, select a circle, make it smaller place it on the left side of the top piece of the acorn, and then duplicate the circle and place it on the right side. Select the acorn and click 'weld'.

Turn back on all of the other pieces of the design, resize the width to 11.5 inches, select the entire design, click 'attach', and then tap 'Make It'. Mirror the design in the mat preview screen and click 'continue'. Set your material to Heat transfer vinyl and tools too. Place the heat transfer vinyl with the shiny side down on a mat and put it in the Cricut to cut. After cutting, remove the mat from the machine, flip the mat over, and peel the mat away from the heat transfer vinyl. Trim the excess vinyl with scissors and weed your design. Turn on the easy press and preheat to about 330°F for 30 seconds

Preheat the pillow cover to remove any wrinkles or any moisture. Put the pillow cover with the zipper at the bottom and place your design on it. Put a Teflon sheet on top of the design and press for 30 seconds. Move the easy press over and press the rest of the design for an additional 30 seconds.

Let the design cool down for a few minutes and then peel off the carrier sheet.

Customized Tablecloths

Materials Needed

- o   Linen or cotton tablecloth
- o   Cricut Maker 3 smart cutting machine
- o   Cricut Smart Stencil material
- o   Weeding tool and scraper
- o   Transfer tape
- o   Fabric paint
- o   Paintbrush

Instructions

Open a new canvas in the Cricut design space. Go to images and type 'lobster'. Select the image and click 'add to canvas.' Determine the dimensions of your tablecloth, and adjust the size of lobsters and other images. For a consistent pattern, duplicate images to ensure uniform size. When satisfied, click 'Make It'. Set your material- smart stencil and choose 'without mat'. Place the smart stencil into the cutting machine to cut.

Use a weeding tool to eliminate undesirable elements from the Smart Stencil design before painting, creating a cut-out of the desired design. Apply transfer tape over the stencil to maintain the cohesiveness of all pieces as a unified design, using a scraper to eliminate any potential air bubbles.

Place the transfer tape with the attached stencil on the tablecloth, ensuring it's centered, straight, and crease-free. Use a scraper to apply it, then gently peel back the transfer tape at an angle to unveil the design, leaving the Smart Stencil in place. In a well-ventilated area, apply the fabric paint to your design following the instructions on the bottle. Allow it to dry for a few minutes before delicately peeling away the Smart Stencil. Allow it to dry thoroughly.

Monogrammed Wall Hangings

Materials Needed

- Wall frame
- Cricut machine
- Cricut smart vinyl (Removable)
- Photo mat
- Scissors
- Transfer tape

Instructions.

Open a new canvas in the Cricut design space. Click on images and then image sets. Type 'Motifs'. Search for the 'P' and select the dark blue version of the letter.

Click add to canvas. To split the letter 'P', click on shapes and select a square. Unlock it and make the width 6 inches. Make it 0.25 inch high, and place it strategically a little above half of the letter from the top. Select both, align, and center horizontally. Slice it and take away the part you don't need.

Now, the design is split but still in one piece and it needs to be in separate pieces so I can add the text ' Carole'. Go back to shapes and select a square. Place it in the bottom half, and make sure you are in the center, you don't want to cut off part of your letter. Select both together and slice. Take this away and delete it. Your monogram is in two separate pieces. To add bars across to frame the halves of the monogram, go back to shapes, select a square, and unlock the size to be 6 inches wide. Resize its height to 0.25 inch, place it along the edge of the top, highlight both click align, and then center horizontally.

 Duplicate the first bar, make sure it's lined up, select the two top pieces together, and click 'weld'. Also, select the two bottom pieces and click 'weld'.

To add text, click on the text icon, move it over here, double-click so you can type ' CAROLE' in capital letters in the center, and change the font. Place the text inside the 'P', select all, click align, and then center horizontally. Resize the image to 7 inches wide and 9.5 inches high and then click 'attach'.

Click 'Make It'. You can now see it on your mat preview screen. Mirror the image and select 'without mat'. Click 'continue'. Place the vinyl into the Cricut machine to cut.

After cutting, trim the excess and weed the design. Place transfer tape on top of the design, smooth it down, and peel back the design. Here is my photo mat for my frame and I have used a textured black cardstock behind it. Center the design on the photo mat and ensure it is flat.

Smooth it out and carefully remove the carrier sheet. Ensure that on the small edges, your carrier sheet is not pulling up the vinyl. Put the photo mat back into the frame and hang it at home.

Personalized Door Mats

Materials Needed

- Cricut machine

- o Doormat
- o Freezer paper
- o Flex card
- o Cricut light grip mat
- o Cardstock
- o Cricut easy press

Instructions

Open a new canvas on the Cricut design space. Go to the image library and select a design. Click add to canvas. Resize the design to fit your doormat. Select the design and click 'ungroup' to take out the parts you don't need.

To make a stencil out of the freezer paper, ensure that all the letters have space to align them back up. Select all the letters, click 'align' a, and then 'align bottom'. This will align all the letters straight again. Click 'attach' and then tap 'make it'.On the mat preview screen, turn on the mirror icon because it's a stencil and needs to be cut backward. Select the material - cardstock and tap 'more pressure'

Place the freezer paper shiny side up on the light grip mat and put it in the cutting machine. Turn on the Cricut easy press to preheat. Carefully remove the freezer past stencil from the Cricut mat. Lay the stencil on the doormat and press at 70°F for 45 seconds. Allow it to cool and then start working on the flex seal one letter after another.

Let it dry for a few hours and peel away the freezer paper from the doormat.

DIY Baby Cloth Dividers

Materials Needed

- o 4 pieces of white 80 lb. cardstock
- o 1 piece of paper
- o Cricut blue Light Grip mat
- o Cricut spatula
- o Cricut Access

- o Cricut machine (Explore Air 2 or Maker)
- o Printer

Instructions

Open a new canvas in the Cricut design space and click on 'images'. Type 'door hanger' on the search bar. The Cricut Access subscription becomes essential here; images marked with a green 'a' in the top left corner are exclusive to subscribers, and you can explore the subscription with a 30-day trial.

Choose the door hanger image highlighted with a green square in the provided screenshot. Then, click the 'Insert Images'.Resize your door hanger to a height of 7 inches. In the top left, under Fill, select the icon resembling a smaller version of the door hanger, then scroll down to 'Pattern.' Clicking on 'Pattern' allows you to choose from patterns within the Cricut software, including the floral pattern used for my door hangers.

After selecting your desired pattern, click on 'Edit Pattern' under the 'Fill' area to scale it (I scaled mine to 260) and ensure it fits the image without repeating. Customize your closet dividers by adding design elements like a 'label' at the top for sizes and a 'onesie' on the front. Add text as needed and select the entire design, then click 'Align' and then 'Center Horizontally.'

Click 'Duplicate' seven times and spread out the hanger. Go to the text icon and type the sizes(NB, 0-3months, 3-6monthsh, 6-9monthsh, 9-12monthsh, 12-18monthsh, 18-24monthsh, 2T) on each of the hangers. Attach two closet dividers (for printing and cutting on a single sheet of cardstock), and then flatten them to create a cohesive design.Click 'Make It'. Set up as a 'Print and then cut, click 'continue', send it to the printer, and print each sheet of closet dividers. The black squares around them will be printed as score lines, guiding your Cricut machine in precise cutting.

Ensure to choose 'Add Bleed' during the cutting process. This ensures that your printer extends the design and ink slightly beyond the actual outline.

As a result, when the Cricut cuts it, your design will cover the entire front of your closet divider. After printing on your four sheets of cardstock, they will appear like this.

Set the material to cardstock. Place your cardstock on the blue Light Grip mat (you can also use a brayer to help secure it to the mat if you're worried about getting the white cardstock dirty with your fingers) and cut! After cutting, remove the mat from the machine, and detach the cardstock from your mat by flipping it and peeling it away from the cardstock. Your cloth hanger divider is ready!

Chapter 17

Troubleshooting and Tips

Common Issues and Solutions: A troubleshooting guide for common problems.

Common Cricut Design Space issues include:

Problem 1: Receiving a 404-HTTP error notification.

Solution: Clear cookies and caches. If the issue persists, try using a different search engine like Mozilla Firefox, Bing, or Safari. Attempt to open Design Space on another computer. If the problem persists, contact the company's Member Care team for assistance.

Problem 2: If you encounter a (-2) error while sending a project to your Cricut machine, indicating a 'Not Supported' message.

Solution: Use the Explore or Maker model for your project, as other machines may not be compatible with the software.

Confirm your web browser is up to date; consider trying another search engine to see if the app opens.

Ensure your software meets the system requirements necessary to run the Cricut software.

Cricut Explore & Maker Machines Troubleshooting

Explore the common problems related to Cricut Explore a series of machines and discover solutions for them:

Problem 1: Unusual Noises from My Cricut Maker/Explore Machine

Solution: Examine the machine for any physical damage. Confirm that you are using the correct power cord provided with the machine. If the problem persists after completing these steps, promptly contact Member Care and report your concern.

Problem 2: Cricut Machine Tearing or Dragging Material

Solution: To address the problem of your Cricut machine tearing or dragging through the material, implement the following steps:

Confirm the correct material setting in Design Space.

Double-check the image size and complexity, or inspect the blade housing for debris.

Consider replacing the blade and mat, as either could be contributing to the issue.

Cricut Joy Model Troubleshooting

In addition to the Design Space app, Maker, or Explore models, the Cricut Joy model encounters its own set of issues.

Problem 1: Continuous Rolling of Cricut Joy Roller Bar

Solution: This problem may result from interference with mat/material sensors. Address it by following these steps:

Turn off and unplug the machine. Clean the machine sensors using compressed air or a microfiber cloth. If the issue persists after cleaning the sensors, contact Member Care for assistance.

Problem 2: Machine Not Cutting Through Material

Solution: If your machine is struggling to cut through the loaded material: Confirm the appropriate cut setting for the selected material.

Verify that the blade housing is properly seated on the clamp.

Cricut Mug Press Troubleshooting

For those encountering issues with the Mug Press, particularly in the connection process.

Problem 1: Correct Way to Connect With Press

Solution: To connect the Mug Press for design creation, ensure the power cord is connected to both the press and the outlet. Switch on the press; it should flash orange. Connect the USB cable to both the press and the computer.

Problem 2: Preventing Black Dots During Mug Pressing

Solution: To avoid black dots during the Mug Press process, ensure a clean environment, trim the Infusible Ink Transfer Sheet liner close to the design, and refrain from working directly in front of fans.

Cricut Auto Press Troubleshooting

Problem 1: Eliminating Press Marks on Projects

Solution: Open the blank and slide it over the mat or platen to have only one layer of the base material on the mat. Additionally, place a pressing pillow inside the blank to elevate and support the pressing area.

Problem 2: Auto Press Not Powering On After Plugging in.

Solution: Ensure the power cord is correctly inserted into the right wall outlet. If the issue persists, try another wall outlet to rule out potential machine errors. If these steps prove ineffective, contact the Member Care team for further assistance.

Cricut Heat Press Troubleshooting

While operating the electric Heat Press, address the following common issues:

Problem 1: Heat Press Automatically Turning Off.

Solution: The Cricut Heat Press is designed with an Auto-Shut Off feature, turning off after 13 minutes of inactivity. This is a built-in function, so there's no need for concern.

Problem 2: Blinking Heat Wave Lights on Heat Press

Solution: If the Heat Wave lights on your Heat Press are blinking red or orange, it signals an error. To resolve this, unplug the press cable for at least 30 seconds and then reconnect it to observe the results.

Problem 1: Your Cricut machine may not recognize the material or mat due to various reasons.

Solution: Dirty sensors or mat: Clean the machine's sensors gently with a soft cloth or compressed air. Ensure the mat is clean and free of debris.

Damaged or worn mat: Inspect the cutting mat for damage or excessive wear. Replace it if necessary.

Compatibility issues: Confirm you are using a mat and material compatible with your specific Cricut machine model.

Firmware or software updates: Ensure your machine's firmware and software are up-to-date to prevent recognition issues.

Sensor calibration: Calibrate your Cricut machine according to the provided steps for your specific model.

Incorrect material setting: Double-check the material setting in Cricut Design Space to ensure it matches the actual material you're using. Incorrect settings can lead to recognition problems.

Cricut Maintenance: Tips for maintaining your machine.

Similar to any device, your Cricut cutter requires regular maintenance to ensure it cuts effectively and operates seamlessly. Understanding the necessary maintenance tasks and their recommended frequency is crucial for maintaining optimal machine functionality.

Maintaining your Cricut cutting machine is straightforward and doesn't require much time. The primary task is thorough cleaning to eliminate material, fiber, and dust buildup, ensuring the rollers, mats, and carriage move freely. Clean both the interior and exterior using tools like glass cleaner, a soft cloth, a small bristle brush, and, for effective cleaning, a vacuum with a small attachment or compressed air can be beneficial.

To clean your Cricut machine, follow these steps that can be applied to any model: Unplug your Cricut. Disconnect the plug from both the back of the machine and the wall. If you use a USB cable, unplug it as well.

Remove Dust & Debris

Eliminate lint, dust, fibers, and debris by employing compressed air and a detailed vacuum attachment. Begin by directing compressed air inside the machine to expel particles outward. Use the vacuum to remove visible dirt, employing a soft bristle brush, such as a clean toothbrush or paintbrush, for hard-to-reach areas and stubborn spots.

Carriage & Roller bar

For cleaning around the carriage and roller bar, use baby wipes or lightly spray a cloth with glass cleaner. Avoid spraying cleaner directly onto the machine; always spray the cloth to control application. You can make your glass cleaner with 1 part vinegar, 1 part water, and a few drops of dish soap. Never use acetone (e.g., nail polish remover) on your machine. Remove any blades, clean around the carriage, slide star wheels to one side on the roller bar, and wipe it down along with the area under the carriage and carriage shaft using a soft cloth or baby wipe.

If you observe grease buildup on the carriage shaft, gently use a Q-tip or tissue to remove it. If re-greasing is needed, contact Cricut support for complete instructions. Wipe the carriage, open clamp A and clamp B gently, avoiding contact with the gearing on the Cricut Maker and Maker 3.

Clean the Inside & outside of The Machine

Clean inside your Maker or Explore machine by wiping down storage compartments with a soft cloth or baby wipe. Wipe the bottom tray, the inside of the lid, and the rear slot. Ensure thorough inspection to remove all dirt from visible surfaces, except those not recommended for cleaning. Wipe the exterior of your Cricut, including storage compartments. For Explore, avoid cleaning inside the cartridge slot

Delicately clean the buttons and (on the Explore model) the dial, ensuring the cloth or wipe is not excessively damp to prevent liquid from seeping around the buttons.

Afterward, shut the machine and wipe the front of the tray and the lid's top.

Eliminate debris by blowing out the USB slot and the AC plug slot.

Allow your machine to air dry completely upon opening before engaging in crafting or storage.

Clean The Cutting Mats

Begin the process of restoring your cutting mat by cleaning it; cleaning alone might be sufficient. After cleaning, check if the mat has regained its stickiness, and consider trying these methods first.

Several methods can be employed to clean your mat. Some of these include:

Using Soap & Water

To clean your cutting mat affordably and effortlessly, start with the soap and water method, as recommended by Cricut. Consider skipping soap if it proves unnecessary. Begin by using tweezers to remove large debris, avoiding scraping as it may embed debris further into the mat.

Rinse the mat under lukewarm water, either by running water over it or placing it in a nearby bowl. Use a plastic, hard-bristled brush to gently scrub the mat in circular motions, or use your hands for a more cautious approach. Pat the mat dry with a paper towel, ensuring debris is completely removed. Allow it to air dry for 1-2 hours. For more stubborn messes, consider using soaps like Dawn.

Using Baby Wipes

Use alcohol-free baby wipes to gently clean the mat's surface without compromising the adhesive. Wipe the mat in a circular motion until the entire surface is clean. For heavily soiled mats, multiple wipes may be necessary. Apply gentle pressure to avoid scratching off the adhesive. Ensure the mat is completely air-dried before using it.

Using Lint Roller

Use a lint roller to eliminate small remnants of material stuck to the mat. Roll it over the mat's surface to pick up tiny paper pieces, glitter, or fuzzies effectively.

Using the Cricut Scraper Tool

Use the plastic Cricut scraper tool, preferably the XL scraper, to remove large pieces of leftover material or debris. Gently glide the scraper tool's edge over the cutting mat's surface to dislodge small fragments of excess material, stray hair, or fuzz.

Using Goo Gone

For stubborn build-up, consider using Goo Gone. Apply a small amount onto your cutting mat, spread it with a paper towel, and allow it to settle for 15 minutes. Use a scraper or an old credit card to remove the debris. Wash the mat afterward to ensure complete removal of the goo.

Regardless of the cleaning method you choose, ensure the mat air-dries completely. Place it on a drying rack or hang it vertically. Avoid using heat, as it can damage the mat. Refrain from wiping it with a towel to prevent adding more fuzz and lint to the sticky surface you're trying to eliminate.

After cleaning and drying the mat, check its stickiness. If it remains non-sticky, you may need to restick your cutting mat.

Clean the Blades

For the premium fine point, deep cut, and bonded fabric blades, clean by puncturing a tin foil ball multiple times to remove residue and debris; however, note that this method doesn't sharpen the blade despite some claims.

Use rubbing alcohol on a cotton ball to clean other blades and tools, effectively removing adhesive residue and drying quickly. Exercise extreme caution when cleaning knife blades and rotary blades due to their sharpness. This approach is also suitable for fine, deep, and bonded fabric blades.

Regularly clean both the blades and mats, as a dirty blade or mat is a common cause of imperfect and incomplete cuts.

How Often Should the Cricut Machine Be Cleaned?

If you use your Cricut regularly, especially for cardstock and paper, clean the cutter every 3 months; otherwise, every 6 months should suffice. If your machine has been in storage, clean it before use to eliminate any accumulated dust.

About the Author

Linda C. Brown is an accomplished DIY enthusiast and creative entrepreneur with a passion for crafting and design. With years of experience in utilizing cutting-edge technology to bring her visions to life, Linda has become a leading expert in the world of Cricut crafting.

Driven by her desire to empower others to unleash their creativity, Linda has dedicated herself to simplifying the intricate world of Cricut crafting for beginners. Her innovative approach combines straightforward techniques with imaginative design concepts, making it easier than ever for novices to embark on their crafting journey.

Through her clear and concise instructions, Linda's goal is to equip readers with the skills and confidence needed to create stunning projects with the Cricut Maker 3. From personalized gifts to profitable ventures, her book, "No-Fluff Beginner's Guide to Cricut Maker 3 Projects," serves as the ultimate resource for anyone looking to dive into the world of DIY crafting.

Linda C. Brown's expertise extends beyond the pages of her book, as she continues to inspire and educate through workshops, tutorials, and online communities. Her infectious enthusiasm and unwavering commitment to creativity have earned her a dedicated following of crafters eager to explore the limitless possibilities of the Cricut Maker 3.

Made in the USA
Columbia, SC
23 October 2024

44913082R00220